∴ *The Yale Shakespeare* ∴

THE TRAGEDY OF CORIOLANUS

EDITED BY

TUCKER BROOKE

NEW HAVEN · YALE UNIVERSITY PRESS

LONDON · GEOFFREY CUMBERLEGE

OXFORD UNIVERSITY PRESS

TABLE OF CONTENTS

The facsimile opposite reproduces from a copy in the Yale University Library the title-page of Nahum Tate's version of 'Coriolanus,' the earliest separate edition of the play in any form.   (See p. 164.)

THE
INGRATITUDE

OF A

Common-Wealth:

Or, the FALL of

Caius Martius Coriolanus.

Caius martius Coriolanus

As IT IS

ACTED

AT THE

Theatre - Royal.

By N. Tate.

——Honoratum si forte reponis Achillem,
Impiger, Iracundus, Inexorabilis, Acer,
Jura neget sibi nata, nihil non arroget Armis.   Hor.

LONDON,
Printed by T. M. for *Joseph Hindmarsh,* at the *Black-Bull*
in *Cornhill.* 1 6 8 2.

[DRAMATIS PERSONÆ

CAIUS MARTIUS, *later named* CORIOLANUS
COMINIUS ⎱ *Roman Generals*
TITUS LARTIUS ⎰
MENENIUS AGRIPPA, *Friend to Coriolanus*
SICINIUS VELUTUS ⎱ *Tribunes of the People*
JUNIUS BRUTUS ⎰
YOUNG MARTIUS, *Son to Coriolanus*
A Roman Herald
TULLUS AUFIDIUS, *General of the Volscians*
Lieutenant to Aufidius
Conspirators with Aufidius
A Roman, *named Nicanor*
A Volscian, *named Adrian*
A Citizen of Antium
Two Volscian Guards

VOLUMNIA, *Mother to Coriolanus*
VIRGILIA, *Wife to Coriolanus*
VALERIA, *A noble lady of Rome*
Gentlewoman, *attendant of Virgilia*

Roman and Volscian Senators, Patricians, Ædiles, Lictors, Soldiers, Citizens, Messengers, Servants to Aufidius, and other Attendants.

SCENE: *Rome and the Volscian country to the south, with the towns of Corioli and Antium.*]

The Tragedy of Coriolanus

ACT FIRST

Scene One

[Rome. A Street]

Enter a Company of mutinous Citizens, with staves, clubs, and other weapons.

1. Cit. Before we proceed any further, hear me speak.

All. Speak, speak.

1. Cit. You are all resolved rather to die than   4
to famish?

All. Resolved, resolved.

1. Cit. First, you know Caius Martius is chief
enemy to the people.   8

All. We know 't, we know 't.

1. Cit. Let us kill him, and we'll have corn at
our own price. Is 't a verdict?

All. No more talking on 't; let it be done. 12
Away, away!

2. Cit. One word, good citizens.

1. Cit. We are accounted poor citizens, the
patricians good. What authority surfeits on 16
would relieve us. If they would yield us but
the superfluity, while it were wholesome, we
might guess they relieved us humanely; but
they think we are too dear: the leanness that 20
afflicts us, the object of our misery, is as an
inventory to particularise their abundance; our

19 guess: *think*   20 are too dear: *cost too much*
21 object: *spectacle*   22 particularise: *itemize*

sufferance is a gain to them. Let us revenge
this with our pikes, ere we become rakes: for 24
the gods know I speak this in hunger for bread,
not in thirst for revenge.

2. Cit. Would you proceed especially against
Caius Martius?   28

All. Against him first: he's a very dog to the
commonalty.

2. Cit. Consider you what services he has done
for his country?   32

1. Cit. Very well; and could be content to
give him good report for 't, but that he pays
himself with being proud.

2. Cit. Nay, but speak not maliciously.   36

1. Cit. I say unto you, what he hath done
famously, he did it to that end: though soft-
conscienced men can be content to say it was
for his country, he did it to please his mother, 40
and to be partly proud; which he is, even to the
altitude of his virtue.

2. Cit. What he cannot help in his nature, you
account a vice in him. You must in no way say 44
he is covetous.

1. Cit. If I must not, I need not be barren of
accusations: he hath faults, with surplus, to tire
in repetition. *Shouts within.* What shouts are 48
these? The other side o' the city is risen: why
stay we prating here? to the Capitol!

All. Come, come.

1. Cit. Soft! who comes here?   52

Enter Menenius Agrippa.

23 sufferance: *suffering*   36 2. Cit.; *cf. n.*
41 to be partly: *in part in order to be*
47, 48 to . . . repetition: *which it would weary one to list over*

2. Cit. Worthy Menenius Agrippa; one that
hath always loved the people.

1. Cit. He's one honest enough: would all the
rest were so!   56

Men. What work's, my countrymen, in hand? Where
go you
With bats and clubs? The matter? Speak, I pray
you.

2. Cit. Our business is not unknown to the
senate; they have had inkling this fortnight what 60
we intend to do, which now we'll show 'em in
deeds. They say poor suitors have strong
breaths: they shall know we have strong arms
too.   64

Men. Why, masters, my good friends, mine honest
neighbours,
Will you undo yourselves?

2. Cit. We cannot, sir; we are undone
already.   68

Men. I tell you, friends, most charitable care
Have the patricians of you. For your wants,
Your suffering in this dearth, you may as well
Strike at the heaven with your staves as lift them 72
Against the Roman state, whose course will on
The way it takes, cracking ten thousand curbs
Of more strong link asunder than can ever
Appear in your impediment. For the dearth,   76
The gods, not the patricians, make it, and
Your knees to them, not arms, must help. Alack!
You are transported by calamity
Thither where more attends you; and you slander   80
The helms o' the state, who care for you like fathers,
When you curse them as enemies.

---

58 bats: *heavy sticks*   74 curbs: *restraining chains*
80 more: *more calamity*   81 helms: *pilots*

2. Cit. Care for us! True, indeed! They
ne'er cared for us yet: suffer us to famish, and 84
their storehouses crammed with grain; make
edicts for usury, to support usurers; repeal
daily any wholesome act established against the
rich, and provide more piercing statutes daily 88
to chain up and restrain the poor. If the wars
eat us not up, they will; and there's all the love
they bear us.

Men. Either you must   92
Confess yourselves wondrous malicious,
Or be accus'd of folly. I shall tell you
A pretty tale: it may be you have heard it;
But, since it serves my purpose, I will venture   96
To scale 't a little more.

2. Cit. Well, I'll hear it, sir; yet you must not
think to fob off our disgrace with a tale; but,
an 't please you, deliver.   100

Men. There was a time when all the body's members
Rebell'd against the belly; thus accus'd it:
That only like a gulf it did remain
I' the midst o' the body, idle and unactive,   104
Still cupboarding the viand, never bearing
Like labour with the rest, where th' other instruments
Did see and hear, devise, instruct, walk, feel,
And, mutually participate, did minister   108
Unto the appetite and affection common
Of the whole body. The belly answer'd,—

2. Cit. Well, sir, what answer made the
belly?   112

Men. Sir, I shall tell you.—With a kind of smile,
Which ne'er came from the lungs, but even thus—

---

97 scale 't; *cf. n.*   99 disgrace: *unfavored treatment*
103 gulf: *devouring whirlpool*   108 participate: *cooperating*
114 Which . . . lungs; *cf. n.*

For, look you, I may make the belly smile
As well as speak—it taintingly replied   116
To the discontented members, the mutinous parts
That envied his receipt; even so most fitly
As you malign our senators for that
They are not such as you.
    2. Cit.   Your belly's answer?   What! 120
The kingly crowned head, the vigilant eye,
The counsellor heart, the arm our soldier,
Our steed the leg, the tongue our trumpeter,
With other muniments and petty helps   124
In this our fabric, if that they—
    Men.   What then?—
'Fore me, this fellow speaks! what then? what then?
    2. Cit. Should by the cormorant belly be restrain'd,
Who is the sink o' the body,—
    Men.   Well, what then? 128
    2. Cit. The former agents, if they did complain,
What could the belly answer?
    Men.   I will tell you;
If you'll bestow a small, of what you have little,
Patience a while, you'st hear the belly's answer.   132
    2. Cit. You're long about it.
    Men.   Note me this, good friend;
Your most grave belly was deliberate,
Not rash like his accusers, and thus answer'd:
'True is it, my incorporate friends,' quoth he,   136
'That I receive the general food at first,
Which you do live upon; and fit it is,
Because I am the store-house and the shop

116 taintingly: *effectively; cf. n.*
118 his receipt: *what he received*
124 muniments: *furnishings*
128 sink: *cesspool*
133 Note me: *pray note*
139 shop: *workshop*

122 counsellor heart; *cf. n.*
126 'Fore me: *by my faith!*
132 you'st: *you shall*
136 incorporate: *joined in one body*

Of the whole body: but, if you do remember,   140
I send it through the rivers of your blood,
Even to the court, the heart, to the seat o' the brain;
And, through the cranks and offices of man,
The strongest nerves and small inferior veins   144
From me receive that natural competency
Whereby they live. And though that all at once,
You, my good friends,'—this says the belly, mark
    me,—

  2. Cit. Ay, sir; well, well.

  Men.   'Though all at once cannot 148
See what I do deliver out to each,
Yet I can make my audit up, that all
From me do back receive the flour of all,
And leave me but the bran.' What say you to 't?   152

  2. Cit. It was an answer: how apply you this?

  Men. The senators of Rome are this good belly,
And you the mutinous members; for, examine
Their counsels and their cares, digest things rightly 156
Touching the weal o' the common, you shall find
No public benefit which you receive
But it proceeds or comes from them to you,
And no way from yourselves. What do you think, 160
You, the great toe of this assembly?

  2. Cit. I the great toe? Why the great toe?

  Men. For that, being one o' the lowest, basest,
    poorest,
Of this most wise rebellion, thou go'st foremost: 164
Thou rascal, that art worst in blood to run,
Lead'st first to win some vantage.

---

143 cranks: *winding passages*   offices: *kitchen, etc.*
145 competency: *sufficiency*
157 weal . . . common: *common weal*
165 rascal . . . blood; *cf. n.*
166 Lead'st first: *art the very leader*   vantage: *personal profit*

But make you ready your stiff bats and clubs:
Rome and her rats are at the point of battle;   168
The one side must have bale.

Enter Caius Martius.

                              Hail, noble Martius!
  Mar. Thanks.—What's the matter, you dissentious
      rogues,
That, rubbing the poor itch of your opinion,
Make yourselves scabs?
  2. Cit.   We have ever your good word. 172
  Mar. He that will give good words to thee will
      flatter
Beneath abhorring. What would you have, you curs,
That like nor peace nor war? the one affrights you,
The other makes you proud. He that trusts to you, 176
Where he should find you lions, finds you hares;
Where foxes, geese: you are no surer, no,
Than is the coal of fire upon the ice,
Or hailstone in the sun. Your virtue is,   180
To make him worthy whose offence subdues him,
And curse that justice did it. Who deserves greatness
Deserves your hate; and your affections are
A sick man's appetite, who desires most that   184
Which would increase his evil. He that depends
Upon your favours swims with fins of lead
And hews down oaks with rushes. Hang ye! Trust
      ye?
With every minute you do change a mind,   188
And call him noble that was now your hate,

---

169 bale: *disaster*   171, 172 rubbing . . . scabs; *cf. n.*
174 Beneath abhorring: *more than can be enough abhorred*
175 nor . . . nor: *neither . . . nor*   179 *Cf. n.*
180-182 Your virtue . . . did it; *cf. n.*
183 affections: *favorable opinions*

Him vile that was your garland. What's the matter,
That in these several places of the city
You cry against the noble senate, who,   192
Under the gods, keep you in awe, which else
Would feed on one another? What's their seeking?

Men. For corn at their own rates; whereof they say
The city is well stor'd.

Mar.   Hang 'em! They say!   196
They'll sit by the fire, and presume to know
What's done i' the Capitol; who's like to rise,
Who thrives, and who declines; side factions, and give
    out
Conjectural marriages; making parties strong,   200
And feebling such as stand not in their liking
Below their cobbled shoes. They say there's grain
    enough!
Would the nobility lay aside their ruth,
And let me use my sword, I'd make a quarry   204
With thousands of these quarter'd slaves, as high
As I could pick my lance.

Men. Nay, these are almost thoroughly persuaded;
For though abundantly they lack discretion,   208
Yet are they passing cowardly. But, I beseech you,
What says the other troop?

Mar.   They are dissolv'd: hang 'em!
They said they were an-hungry; sigh'd forth proverbs:
That hunger broke stone walls; that dogs must eat;   212
That meat was made for mouths; that the gods sent not
Corn for the rich men only. With these shreds
They vented their complainings; which being answer'd,

198 like: *likely*   199 side: *espouse*
200 parties: *favored factions*   201 feebling: *reducing*
204 quarry: *pile of dead*   206 pick: *pitch*
209 passing: *surpassingly*
215 vented: *gave vent to*   answer'd: *satisfied*

And a petition granted them, a strange one,—   216
To break the heart of generosity,
And make bold power look pale,—they threw their
      caps
As they would hang them on the horns o' the moon,
Shouting their emulation.
    Men.   What is granted them? 220
    Mar. Five tribunes to defend their vulgar wisdoms,
Of their own choice: one's Junius Brutus,
Sicinius Velutus, and I know not—'Sdeath!
The rabble should have first unroof'd the city,   224
Ere so prevail'd with me; it will in time
Win upon power, and throw forth greater themes
For insurrection's arguing.
    Men.   This is strange.
    Mar. Go; get you home, you fragments!   228

                Enter a Messenger, hastily.

    Mess. Where's Caius Martius?
    Mar.   Here: what's the matter?
    Mess. The news is, sir, the Volsces are in arms.
    Mar. I am glad on 't; then we shall ha' means to
      vent
Our musty superfluity.   See, our best elders.   232

Enter Sicinius Velutus, Junius Brutus; Cominius,
      Titus Lartius, with other Senators.

    1. Sen. Martius, 'tis true that you have lately told
      us;
The Volsces are in arms.
    Mar.   They have a leader,

217 generosity: *the gentry*
226 Win upon: *get ahead of*   power: *constituted authority*
227 For . . . arguing: *for insurgents to maintain*
231 vent: *dispose of*

Tullus Aufidius, that will put you to 't.
I sin in envying his nobility,   236
And were I anything but what I am,
I would wish me only he.

    Com.   You have fought together.

    Mar. Were half to half the world by th' ears, and he
Upon my party, I'd revolt, to make   240
Only my wars with him: he is a lion
That I am proud to hunt.

    1. Sen.   Then, worthy Martius,
Attend upon Cominius to these wars.

    Com. It is your former promise.

    Mar.   Sir, it is;   244
And I am constant.   Titus Lartius, thou
Shalt see me once more strike at Tullus' face.
What! art thou stiff? stand'st out?

    Tit.   No, Caius Martius;
I'll lean upon one crutch and fight with t'other,   248
Ere stay behind this business.

    Men.   O! true-bred.

    Sen. Your company to the Capitol; where I know
Our greatest friends attend us.

    Tit.   [*To Cominius.*] Lead you on:
[*To Martius.*] Follow Cominius; we must follow
    you;   252
Right worthy you priority.

    Com.   Noble Martius!

    Sen. [*To the Citizens.*] Hence! to your homes! be
    gone.

    Mar.   Nay, let them follow:
The Volsces have much corn; take these rats thither
To gnaw their garners.   Worshipful mutiners,   256

239 half to half: *one half against the other*
241 Only . . . with him: *with him alone*
247 stand'st out: *do you decline to go?*

Your valour puts well forth; pray, follow.

   Exeunt [Martius, Cominius, Titus, etc.]. Citi-
             zens steal away.

      Mane[n]t Sicin. & Brutus.

Sic. Was ever man so proud as is this Martius?

Bru. He has no equal.   259

Sic. When we were chosen tribunes for the people,—

Bru. Mark'd you his lip and eyes?

Sic.   Nay, but his taunts.

Bru. Being mov'd, he will not spare to gird the gods.

Sic. Bemock the modest moon.

Bru. The present wars devour him! he is grown 264
Too proud to be so valiant.

Sic.   Such a nature,
Tickled with good success, disdains the shadow
Which he treads on at noon. But I do wonder
His insolence can brook to be commanded 268
Under Cominius.

Bru.   Fame, at the which he aims,
In whom already he's well grac'd, cannot
Better be held nor more attain'd than by
A place below the first; for what miscarries 272
Shall be the general's fault, though he perform
To th' utmost of a man; and giddy censure
Will then cry out of Martius 'O! if he
Had borne the business.'

Sic.   Besides, if things go well, 276
Opinion, that so sticks on Martius, shall
Of his demerits rob Cominius.

Bru.   Come:
Half all Cominius' honours are to Martius,

---

257 puts . . . forth: *shows well* (*ironic*)
257 S. d. Manent: *remain on the stage*
265 to be: *of being*   266, 267 disdains . . . noon; *cf. n.*
274 giddy censure: *fickle opinion*   278 demerits: *merits*

Though Martius earn'd them not; and all his faults 280
To Martius shall be honours, though indeed
In aught he merit not.
    Sic.   Let's hence and hear
How the dispatch is made; and in what fashion,
More than his singularity, he goes   284
Upon this present action.
    Bru.   Let's along.   *Exeunt.*

Scene Two

[Corioli. The Senate-house]

Enter Tullus Aufidius with Senators of Corioli.

    1. Sen. So your opinion is, Aufidius,
That they of Rome are enter'd in our counsels,
And know how we proceed.
    Auf.   Is it not yours?
What ever have been thought on in this state,   4
That could be brought to bodily act ere Rome
Had circumvention? 'Tis not four days gone
Since I heard thence; these are the words: I think
I have the letter here; yes, here it is.   8
'They have press'd a power, but it is not known
Whether for east, or west: the dearth is great;
The people mutinous; and it is rumour'd,
Cominius, Martius, your old enemy,—   12
Who is of Rome worse hated than of you,—
And Titus Lartius, a most valiant Roman,
These three lead on this preparation
Whither 'tis bent: most likely 'tis for you: 16
Consider of it.'

---

284 singularity: *peculiar character*   2 enter'd: *instructed*
4 What: *what designs*   6 circumvention: *means to circumvent*
9 press'd a power: *levied troops*   15 preparation: *expedition*

 1. Sen.   Our army's in the field:
We never yet made doubt but Rome was ready
To answer us.
 Auf.   Nor did you think it folly
To keep your great pretences veil'd till when   20
They needs must show themselves; which in the hatch-
  ing,
It seem'd, appear'd to Rome. By the discovery
We shall be shorten'd in our aim, which was
To take in many towns ere almost Rome   24
Should know we were afoot.
 2. Sen.   Noble Aufidius,
Take your commission; hie you to your bands;
Let us alone to guard Corioli:
If they set down before 's, for the remove   28
Bring up your army; but I think you'll find
They've not prepar'd for us.
 Auf.   O! doubt not that;
I speak from certainties. Nay, more;
Some parcels of their power are forth already,   32
And only hitherward. I leave your honours.
If we and Caius Martius chance to meet,
'Tis sworn between us we shall ever strike
Till one can do no more.
 All.   The gods assist you!   36
 Auf. And keep your honours safe!
 1. Sen.   Farewell.
 2. Sen.   Farewell.
 All. Farewell.   *Exeunt omnes.*

20 pretences: *designs*   24 take in : *capture*
27 Corioli; *cf. n.*   28 remove: *raising the siege*
32 parcels: *portions*

Scene Three

[*Rome.   A Room in Martius's House*]

Enter Volumnia and Virgilia, mother and wife to Martius.   They set them down on two low stools and sew.

Vol. I pray you, daughter, sing; or express yourself in a more comfortable sort. If my son were my husband, I should freelier rejoice in that absence wherein he won honour than in the 4 embracements of his bed where he would show most love. When yet he was but tender-bodied and the only son of my womb, when youth with comeliness plucked all gaze his way, when for a 8 day of kings' entreaties a mother should not sell him an hour from her beholding, I, considering how honour would become such a person, that it was no better than picture-like to hang by the 12 wall, if renown made it not stir, was pleased to let him seek danger where he was like to find fame. To a cruel war I sent him; from whence he returned, his brows bound with oak. I tell 16 thee, daughter, I sprang not more in joy at first hearing he was a man-child than now in first seeing he had proved himself a man.

Vir. But had he died in the business, madam; 20 how then?

Vol. Then his good report should have been my son; I therein would have found issue. Hear me profess sincerely: had I a dozen sons, each 24 in my love alike, and none less dear than thine and my good Martius, I had rather had eleven

die nobly for their country than one voluptu-
ously surfeit out of action.   28

Enter a Gentlewoman.

Gent. Madam, the Lady Valeria is come to
visit you.

Vir. Beseech you, give me leave to retire myself.

Vol. Indeed, you shall not.   32
Methinks I hear hither your husband's drum,
See him pluck Aufidius down by the hair,
As children from a bear the Volsces shunning him:
Methinks I see him stamp thus, and call thus: 36
'Come on, you cowards! you were got in fear,
Though you were born in Rome.' His bloody brow
With his mail'd hand then wiping, forth he goes,
Like to a harvestman that's task'd to mow   40
Or all or lose his hire.

Vir. His bloody brow! O Jupiter, no blood!

Vol. Away, you fool! it more becomes a man
Than gilt his trophy: the breasts of Hecuba,   44
When she did suckle Hector, look'd not lovelier
Than Hector's forehead when it spit forth blood,
At Grecian sword contemning. Tell Valeria
We are fit to bid her welcome.   48

Exit Gent.

Vir. Heavens bless my lord from fell Aufidius!

Vol. He'll beat Aufidius' head below his knee,
And tread upon his neck.

Enter Valeria with an Usher, and a Gentlewoman.

Val. My ladies both, good day to you.   52

Vol. Sweet madam.

Vir. I am glad to see your ladyship.

---

28 out of action: *in inactivity*   40 task'd: *assigned the task*
44 Than . . . trophy: *than gilding becomes his monument*
47 contemning: *showing defiance*

Val. How do you both? you are manifest housekeepers. What are you sewing here? A 56 fine spot, in good faith. How does your little son?

Vir. I thank your ladyship; well, good madam.

Vol. He had rather see the swords and hear 60 a drum, than look upon his schoolmaster.

Val. O' my word, the father's son; I'll swear 'tis a very pretty boy. O' my troth, I looked upon him o' Wednesday half an hour together: 64 he has such a confirmed countenance. I saw him run after a gilded butterfly; and when he caught it, he let it go again; and after it again; and over and over he comes, and up again; 68 catched it again: or whether his fall enraged him, or how 'twas, he did so set his teeth and tear it; O! I warrant, how he mammocked it!

Vol. One on 's father's moods.   72

Val. Indeed, la, 'tis a noble child.

Vir. A crack, madam.

Val. Come, lay aside your stitchery; I must have you play the idle huswife with me this 76 afternoon.

Vir. No, good madam; I will not out of doors.

Val. Not out of doors!

Vol. She shall, she shall.   80

Vir. Indeed, no, by your patience; I'll not over the threshold till my lord return from the wars.

Vol. Fie! you confine yourself most un- 84

56 housekeepers: *recluses, stay-at-homes*
57 spot: *pattern for embroidery*   65 confirmed: *determined*
66 gilded: *gold-colored*   71 mammocked: *tore in pieces*
72 on 's: *of his*   74 crack: *lively child*
76 play . . . huswife: *idle away your time*

reasonably.   Come; you must go visit the good
lady that lies in.

Vir. I will wish her speedy strength, and visit
her with my prayers; but I cannot go thither. 88

Vol. Why, I pray you?

Vir. 'Tis not to save labour, nor that I want
love.

Val. You would be another Penelope; yet, 92
they say, all the yarn she spun in Ulysses'
absence did but fill Ithaca full of moths.   Come;
I would your cambric were sensible as your
finger, that you might leave pricking it for pity. 96
Come, you shall go with us.

Vir. No, good madam, pardon me; indeed, I
will not forth.

Val. In truth, la, go with me; and I'll tell 100
you excellent news of your husband.

Vir. O, good madam, there can be none yet.

Val. Verily, I do not jest with you; there
came news from him last night.   104

Vir. Indeed, madam?

Val. In earnest, it's true; I heard a senator
speak it.   Thus it is: The Volsces have an army
forth; against whom Cominius the general is 108
gone, with one part of our Roman power: your
lord and Titus Lartius are set down before their
city Corioli; they nothing doubt prevailing and
to make it brief wars.   This is true, on mine 112
honour; and so, I pray, go with us.

Vir. Give me excuse, good madam; I will
obey you in everything hereafter.

Vol. Let her alone, lady: as she is now she 116
will but disease our better mirth.

90 want: *am lacking in*   95 sensible: *sensitive*
114 Give . . . excuse: *pardon*   117 disease: *disturb*

Val. In troth, I think she would. Fare you
well then. Come, good sweet lady. Prithee,
Virgilia, turn thy solemness out o' door, and go 120
along with us.

Vir. No, at a word, madam; indeed I must
not. I wish you much mirth.

Val. Well then, farewell. *Exeunt Ladies.*

Scene Four

[*Before Corioli*]

*Enter Martius, Titus Lartius, with Drum and Colours,
with Captains and Soldiers, as before the City
Corioli: to them a Messenger.*

Mar. Yonder comes news: a wager they have met.
Lart. My horse to yours, no.
Mar. 'Tis done.
Lart. Agreed.
Mar. Say, has our general met the enemy?
Mess. They lie in view, but have not spoke as yet. 4
Lart. So the good horse is mine.
Mar. I'll buy him of you.
Lart. No, I'll nor sell nor give him; lend you him
I will
For half a hundred years. Summon the town.
Mar. How far off lie these armies?
Mess. Within this mile and half. 8
Mar. Then shall we hear their 'larum, and they ours.
Now, Mars, I prithee, make us quick in work,
That we with smoking swords may march from hence,
To help our fielded friends! Come, blow thy blast. 12

120 turn . . . door: *banish gravity*   122 at a word: *positively*
4 spoke: *euphemism for 'fought'*
12 fielded: *engaged on the battlefield*

*They sound a Parley. Enter two Senators with others
on the Walls of Corioli.*

Tullus Aufidius, is he within your walls?

1. Sen. No, nor a man that fears you less than he:
That's lesser than a little.

               Drum afar off.
             Hark, our drums
Are bringing forth our youth: we'll break our walls, 16
Rather than they shall pound us up: our gates,
Which yet seem shut, we have but pinn'd with rushes;
They'll open of themselves.   Hark you, far off!
               Alarum far off.
There is Aufidius: list, what work he makes   20
Amongst your cloven army.

Mar.   O! they are at it!

Lart. Their noise be our instruction.   Ladders, ho!

Enter the Army of the Volsces.

Mar. They fear us not, but issue forth their city.
Now put your shields before your hearts, and fight 24
With hearts more proof than shields. Advance, brave
    Titus:
They do disdain us much beyond our thoughts,
Which makes me sweat with wrath. Come on, my
    fellows:
He that retires, I'll take him for a Volsce,   28
And he shall feel mine edge.

*Alarum. The Romans are beat back to their trenches.
Enter Martius, cursing.*

Mar. All the contagion of the south light on you, *disease*
You shames of Rome! you herd of—Boils and plagues

14 less; *cf. n.*   17 pound . . . up: *impound, confine*
22 instruction: *directions for proceeding*
26 beyond . . . thoughts: *more than we expected*
30 south: *south wind (thought to bring disease)*

Plaster you o'er, that you may be abhorr'd   32
Further than seen, and one infect another
Against the wind a mile! You souls of geese,
That bear the shapes of men, how have you run
From slaves that apes would beat! Pluto and hell! 36
All hurt behind; backs red, and faces pale
With flight and agu'd fear! Mend and charge home,
Or, by the fires of heaven, I'll leave the foe
And make my wars on you; look to 't: come on;   40
If you'll stand fast, we'll beat them to their wives,
As they us to our trenches follows.

Another alarum, and Martius follows them to gates,
and is shut in.

So, now the gates are ope: now prove good seconds:
'Tis for the followers Fortune widens them,   44
Not for the fliers: mark me, and do the like.

                                        Enter the gates.

   1. Sol. Foolhardiness! not I.
   2. Sol.   Nor I.
                                        Alarum continues.

   1. Sol. See, they have shut him in.
   All.   To the pot, I warrant him.

                    Enter Titus Lartius.

   Lart. What is become of Martius?
   All.   Slain, sir, doubtless. 48
   1. Sol. Following the fliers at the very heels,
With them he enters; who, upon the sudden,
Clapp'd-to their gates; he is himself alone,
To answer all the city.
   Lart.   O noble fellow!   52

34 Against . . . mile; *cf. n.*   38 Mend: *reform*
42 follows; *cf. n.*   43 seconds: *assistants*
47 pot: *cooking-pot; i.e. destruction*   51 himself alone: *quite alone*
52 answer: *withstand*

Who, sensibly, outdares his senseless sword,
And, when it bows, stands up. Thou art left, Martius:
A carbuncle entire, as big as thou art,
Were not so rich a jewel. Thou wast a soldier   56
Even to Cato's wish, not fierce and terrible
Only in strokes; but, with thy grim looks and
The thunder-like percussion of thy sounds,
Thou mad'st thine enemies shake, as if the world   60
Were feverous and did tremble.

Enter Martius, bleeding, assaulted by the Enemy.

1. *Sol.*   Look, sir!
Lart.   O! 'tis Martius!
Let's fetch him off, or make remain alike.
            They fight, and all enter the City.

Scene Five

[*Corioli.   A Street*]

Enter certain Romans, with spoils.

1. *Rom.* This will I carry to Rome.
2. *Rom.* And I this.
3. *Rom.* A murrain on 't! I took this for silver.
            Exeunt.   Alarum continues still afar off.

Enter Martius and Titus, with a Trumpet.

Mar. See here these movers that do prize their
    hours   4
At a crack'd drachme! Cushions, leaden spoons,

---

53 sensibly: *though sensitive to pain*   54 left: *forsaken*
57 Cato's wish; *cf. n.*
62 make . . . alike: *remain to share his fate*   4 movers: *cowards*
5 drachme: *drachma, small Greek coin of silver*

Irons of a doit, doublets that hangmen would
Bury with those that wore them, these base slaves,
Ere yet the fight be done, pack up. Down with
    them! 8
And hark, what noise the general makes! To him!
There is the man of my soul's hate, Aufidius,
Piercing our Romans: then, valiant Titus, take
Convenient numbers to make good the city, 12
Whilst I, with those that have the spirit, will haste
To help Cominius.
    Lart.   Worthy sir, thou bleed'st;
Thy exercise hath been too violent
For a second course of fight.
    Mar.   Sir, praise me not; 16
My work hath yet not warm'd me: fare you well:
The blood I drop is rather physical
Than dangerous to me: to Aufidius thus
I will appear, and fight.
    Lart.   Now the fair goddess, Fortune, 20
Fall deep in love with thee; and her great charms
Misguide thy opposers' swords! Bold gentleman,
Prosperity be thy page!
    Mar.   Thy friend no less
Than those she places highest! So, farewell. 24
    Lart. Thou worthiest Martius!—

                          [*Exit Martius.*]
Go, sound thy trumpet in the market-place;
Call thither all the officers o' the town,
Where they shall know our mind. Away! 28
                            Exeunt.

6 doit: *Dutch copper coin*   6, 7 doublets . . . wore them; *cf. n.*
18 physical: *beneficial to health*
23 Thy friend: *may prosperity befriend thee*

Scene Six

[*Near the Camp of Cominius*]

Enter Cominius as it were in retire, with soldiers.

Com. Breathe you, my friends: well fought; we are
    come off
Like Romans, neither foolish in our stands,
Nor cowardly in retire: believe me, sirs,
We shall be charg'd again.   Whiles we have struck,   4
By interims and conveying gusts we have heard
The charges of our friends.   The Roman gods,
Lead their successes as we wish our own,
That both our powers, with smiling fronts encounter-
    ing,   8
May give you thankful sacrifice.

Enter a Messenger.

                        Thy news?
Mess. The citizens of Corioli have issu'd,
And given to Lartius and to Martius battle:
I saw our party to their trenches driven,   12
And then I came away.
Com.   Though thou speak'st truth,
Methinks thou speak'st not well.   How long is 't since?
Mess. Above an hour, my lord.   15
Com. 'Tis not a mile; briefly we heard their drums:
How couldst thou in a mile confound an hour,
And bring thy news so late?
Mess.   Spies of the Volsces
Held me in chase, that I was forc'd to wheel
Three or four miles about; else had I, sir,   20

5 By . . . gusts: *from time to time, as winds conveyed the sound*
6 The Roman gods; *cf. n.*   16 briefly: *a short time ago*
17 confound: *use up*   19 that: *so that*

Half an hour since brought my report.

　　　　　　　　　Enter Martius [at a distance].

Com.　　　　　　　　　　　　　　Who's yonder,
That does appear as he were flay'd?　O gods!
He has the stamp of Martius; and I have
Before-time seen him thus.

Mar.　　　　　　　　　Come I too late?　　　24

Com. The shepherd knows not thunder from a tabor,
More than I know the sound of Martius' tongue
From every meaner man.

Mar.　　　　　　　　　Come I too late?

Com. Ay, if you come not in the blood of others, 28
But mantled in your own.

Mar.　　　　　　　　　O! let me clip ye
In arms as sound as when I woo'd, in heart
As merry as when our nuptial day was done,
And tapers burnt to bedward.

Com.　　　　　　　　　Flower of warriors. 32
How is 't with Titus Lartius ?

Mar. As with a man busied about decrees:
Condemning some to death, and some to exile;
Ransoming him, or pitying, threat'ning th' other;　36
Holding Corioli in the name of Rome,
Even like a fawning greyhound in the leash,
To let him slip at will.

Com.　　　　　　　　Where is that slave
Which told me they had beat you to your trenches?　40
Where is he?　Call him hither.

Mar.　　　　　　　　　Let him alone;
He did inform the truth: but for our gentlemen,
The common file—a plague! tribunes for them!—

22 as: *as if*　　　　　　　　　　　25 tabor: *small drum*
27 From: *from that of*　　　　　　29 clip: *embrace*
36 pitying: *exempting from ransom*

The mouse ne'er shunn'd the cat as they did budge   44
From rascals worse than they.

 Com.   But how prevail'd you?

 Mar. Will the time serve to tell?   I do not think.
Where is the enemy?   Are you lords o' the field?
If not, why cease you till you are so?   48

 Com. Martius, we have at disadvantage fought,
And did retire to win our purpose.

 Mar. How lies their battle?   Know you on which side
They have plac'd their men of trust?

 Com.   As I guess, Martius, 52
Their bands i' the vaward are the Antiates,
Of their best trust; o'er them Aufidius,
Their very heart of hope.

 Mar.   I do beseech you,
By all the battles wherein we have fought,   56
By the blood we have shed together, by the vows
We have made to endure friends, that you directly
Set me against Aufidius and his Antiates;
And that you not delay the present, but,   60
Filling the air with swords advanc'd and darts,
We prove this very hour.

 Com.   Though I could wish
You were conducted to a gentle bath,
And balms applied to you, yet dare I never   64
Deny your asking: take your choice of those
That best can aid your action.

 Mar.   Those are they
That most are willing.   If any such be here—
As it were sin to doubt—that love this painting   68

---

44 budge: *shrink*
53 vaward: *vanguard* Antiates: *inhabitants of Antium*
58 endure: *continue* 60 delay . . . present: *make present delay*
62 We prove: *that we make trial of*

Wherein you see me smear'd; if any fear
Lesser his person than an ill report;
If any think brave death outweighs bad life,
And that his country's dearer than himself;   72
Let him, alone, or so many so minded,
Wave thus, to express his disposition,
And follow Martius.

> *They all shout, and wave their swords; take*
> *him up in their arms, and cast up their caps.*

[*Soldiers.*] O, me alone! Make you a sword of
  me!   76

[*Mar.*] If these shows be not outward, which of you
But is four Volsces?   None of you but is
Able to bear against the great Aufidius
A shield as hard as his.   A certain number,   80
Though thanks to all, must I select from all: the rest
Shall bear the business in some other fight,
As cause will be obey'd.   Please you to march;
And four shall quickly draw out my command,   84
Which men are best inclin'd.

Com.   March on, my fellows:
Make good this ostentation, and you shall
Divide in all with us.   *Exeunt.*

70 his person: *personal injury*   76 *Cf. n.*
83 As . . . obey'd: *as occasion requires*
86 ostentation: *show of valor*

Scene Seven

[The Gates of Corioli]

*Titus Lartius, having set a guard upon Corioli, going
with drum and trumpet toward Cominius and Caius
Martius, enters with a Lieutenant, other Soldiers,
and a Scout.*

Lart. So; let the ports be guarded: keep your duties,
As I have set them down.   If I do send, dispatch
Those centuries to our aid; the rest will serve
For a short holding: if we lose the field,   4
We cannot keep the town.
Lieu.   Fear not our care, sir.
Lart. Hence, and shut your gates upon 's.
Our guider, come; to the Roman camp conduct us.

Exit.

Scene Eight

*[A Field of Battle between the Roman and the Vol-
scian Camps]*

*Alarum, as in battle.   Enter Martius and Aufidius at
several doors.*

Mar. I'll fight with none but thee; for I do hate thee
Worse than a promise-breaker.
Auf.   We hate alike:
Not Afric owns a serpent I abhor
More than thy fame and envy.   Fix thy foot.   4
Mar. Let the first budger die the other's slave,
And the gods doom him after!
Auf.   If I fly, Martius,

---

1 ports: *gates*   3 centuries: *companies*
(viii) 4 fame and envy: *rivalry in fame (?)*

Halloo me like a hare.

Mar. Within these three hours, Tullus,   8
Alone I fought in your Corioli walls,
And made what work I pleas'd; 'tis not my blood
Wherein thou seest me mask'd; for thy revenge
Wrench up thy power to the highest.

Auf.   Wert thou the Hector 12
That was the whip of your bragg'd progeny,
Thou shouldst not 'scape me here.

> *Here they fight, and certain Volsces come in
> the aid of Aufidius. 'Martius fights till they
> be driven in breathless.*

Officious, and not valiant, you have sham'd me
In your condemned seconds.   16

[*Exit.*]

Scene Nine

[*The Roman Camp*]

*Flourish. Alarum. A retreat is sounded. Enter at
one door Cominius, with the Romans: at another
door Martius, with his arm in a scarf.*

Com. If I should tell thee o'er this thy day's work,
Thou 't not believe thy deeds: but I'll report it
Where senators shall mingle tears with smiles,
Where great patricians shall attend and shrug,   4
I' the end, admire; where ladies shall be frighted,
And, gladly quak'd, hear more; where the dull Trib-
        unes,
That, with the fusty plebeians, hate thine honours,
Shall say, against their hearts,   8

13 whip . . . progeny; *cf. n.*
16 condemned seconds: *despised efforts at assistance*
4 attend: *give attention*   shrug: *express inability to believe*
6 quak'd: *fearful*

'We thank the gods our Rome hath such a soldier!'
Yet cam'st thou to a morsel of this feast,
Having fully din'd before.

    Enter Titus, with his power, from the pursuit.

    Titus Lartius.   O general,
Here is the steed, we the caparison: 12
Hadst thou beheld—

Co. is always compared to an animal

    Mar.   Pray now, no more: my mother,
Who has a charter to extol her blood,
When she does praise me grieves me.   I have done
As you have done; that's what I can: induc'd   16
As you have been; that's for my country:
He that has but effected his good will
Hath overta'en mine act.
    Com.   You shall not be
The grave of your deserving; Rome must know   20
The value of her own: 'twere a concealment
Worse than a theft, no less than a traducement,
To hide your doings; and to silence that,
Which, to the spire and top of praises vouch'd,   24
Would seem but modest.   Therefore, I beseech you,—
In sign of what you are, not to reward
What you have done,—before our army hear me.   27
    Mar. I have some wounds upon me, and they smart
To hear themselves remember'd.
    Com.   Should they not,
Well might they fester 'gainst ingratitude,
And tent themselves with death.   Of all the horses,

12 caparison: *the mere accoutrements*
14 charter: *privilege*   her blood: *him whose blood she shares*
18 effected: *exhibited in action*
20 The grave of: *that which buries or conceals*
23 silence: *ignore with silence*
24 to . . . vouch'd: *testified to with utmost praise*
29 Should they not: *i.e. hear themselves remembered*
31 tent: *cleanse, cure; cf. n.*

Whereof we have ta'en good, and good store, of all 32
The treasure, in this field achiev'd and city,
We render you the tenth; to be ta'en forth,
Before the common distribution,
At your only choice.

    Mar.   I thank you, general;   36
But cannot make my heart consent to take
A bribe to pay my sword: I do refuse it;
And stand upon my common part with those
That have beheld the doing.   40

        A long flourish. They all cry 'Martius! Mar-
           tius!' cast up their caps and lances: Cominius
           and Lartius stand bare.

    Mar. May these same instruments, which you pro-
        fane,
Never sound more! When drums and trumpets shall
I' the field prove flatterers, let courts and cities be
Made all of false-fac'd soothing!   44
When steel grows soft as is the parasite's silk,
Let him be made an overture for the wars!
No more, I say! For that I have not wash'd
My nose that bled, or foil'd some debile wretch,   48
Which, without note, here's many else have done,
You shout me forth
In acclamations hyperbolical;
As if I lov'd my little should be dieted   52
In praises sauc'd with lies.

    Com.   Too modest are you;
More cruel to your good report than grateful
To us that give you truly. By your patience,

32 good store: *a goodly number*
33 in . . . city: *acquired both in this battle and in the city*
40 beheld . . . doing: *been present at the fighting*
44 soothing: *flattery*   46 an overture; *cf. n.*
48 foil'd: *have overcome*   debile: *weak*
49 note: *special attention*   52, 53 dieted In: *fed on*
55 give: *report*

If 'gainst yourself you be incens'd, we'll put you, 56
Like one that means his proper harm, in manacles,
Then reason safely with you. Therefore, be it known,
As to us, to all the world, that Caius Martius
Wears this war's garland; in token of the which, 60
My noble steed, known to the camp, I give him,
With all his trim belonging; and from this time,
For what he did before Corioli, call him,
With all th' applause and clamour of the host, 64
Caius Martius Coriolanus! Bear
The addition nobly ever!
      Flourish. Trumpets sound, and drums.
 Omnes. Caius Martius Coriolanus!
 Cor. I will go wash; 68
And when my face is fair, you shall perceive
Whether I blush, or no: howbeit, I thank you.
I mean to stride your steed, and at all times
To undercrest your good addition 72
To the fairness of my power.
 Com.   So, to our tent;
Where, ere we do repose us, we will write
To Rome of our success. You, Titus Lartius,
Must to Corioli back: send us to Rome 76
The best, with whom we may articulate,
For their own good and ours.
 Lart.   I shall, my lord.
 Cor. The gods begin to mock me. I, that now
Refus'd most princely gifts, am bound to beg 80
Of my lord general.
 Com.   Take 't; 'tis yours. What is 't?
 Cor. I sometime lay here in Corioli

---

57 proper: *own*   60 garland: *i.e. special honor*
62 his . . . belonging: *the trappings that go with him*
66 addition: *title of honor*   69 fair: *clean*
72 undercrest: *maintain as a crest or distinguishing device*
77 articulate: *discuss terms*   82 lay: *lodged*

At a poor man's house; he us'd me kindly:
He cried to me; I saw him prisoner;   84
But then Aufidius was within my view,
And wrath o'erwhelm'd my pity: I request you
To give my poor host freedom.

    Com.   O! well begg'd!
Were he the butcher of my son, he should   88
Be free as is the wind.   Deliver him, Titus.

    Lart. Martius, his name?

    Cor.   By Jupiter! forgot.
I am weary; yea, my memory is tir'd.
Have we no wine here?

    Com.   Go we to our tent: 92
The blood upon your visage dries; 'tis time
It should be look'd to: come.   *Exeunt.*

Scene Ten

[*The Camp of the Volsces*]

*A Flourish.   Cornets.   Enter Tullus Aufidius, bloody,
with two or three Soldiers.*

    Auf. The town is ta'en!

    Sol. 'Twill be deliver'd back on good condition.

    Auf. Condition!
I would I were a Roman; for I cannot,   4
Being a Volsce, be that I am.   Condition!
What good condition can a treaty find
I' the part that is at mercy?   Five times, Martius,
I have fought with thee; so often hast thou beat me, 8
And wouldst do so, I think, should we encounter
As often as we eat.   By th' elements,

2 condition: *terms*   5 that: *what*
7 I': *from the point of view of*

If e'er again I meet him beard to beard,
He is mine, or I am his: mine emulation   12
Hath not that honour in 't it had; for where
I thought to crush him in an equal force—
True sword to sword—I'll potch at him some way
Or wrath or craft may get him.

   Sol.   He's the devil.   16

   Auf. Bolder, though not so subtle.   My valour's
    poison'd
With only suffering stain by him; for him
Shall fly out of itself.   Nor sleep nor sanctuary,
Being naked, sick, nor fane nor Capitol,   20
The prayers of priests, nor times of sacrifice,
Embarquements all of fury, shall lift up
Their rotten privilege and custom 'gainst
My hate to Martius.   Where I find him, were it   24
At home, upon my brother's guard, even there
Against the hospitable canon, would I
Wash my fierce hand in 's heart.   Go you to the city;
Learn how 'tis held, and what they are that must   28
Be hostages for Rome.

   Sol.   Will not you go?

   Auf. I am attended at the cypress grove: I pray
    you—
'Tis south the city mills—bring me word thither
How the world goes, that to the pace of it   32
I may spur on my journey.

   Sol.   I shall, sir.   [*Exeunt.*]

15 potch: *poke, thrust heedlessly*
16 Or wrath: *in which either wrath*
22 Embarquements: *embargoes, restraints*
26 hospitable canon: *law of hospitality*   30 attended: *awaited*

ACT SECOND

Scene One

[Rome. A Public Place]

Enter Menenius, with the two Tribunes of the people, Sicinius & Brutus.

Men. The augurer tells me we shall have news to-night.

Bru. Good or bad?

Men. Not according to the prayer of the people, 4 for they love not Martius.

Sic. Nature teaches beasts to know their friends.

Men. Pray yóu, who does the wolf love? 8

Sic. The lamb.

Men. Ay, to devour him; as the hungry plebeians would the noble Martius.

Bru. He's a lamb indeed, that baes like a 12 bear.

Men. He's a bear indeed, that lives like a lamb. You two are old men; tell me one thing that I shall ask you. 16

Both. Well, sir.

Men. In what enormity is Martius poor in, that you two have not in abundance?

Bru. He's poor in no one fault, but stored 20 with all.

Sic. Especially in pride.

Bru. And topping all others in boasting.

Men. This is strange now: do you two know 24

18 In . . . poor in: *what fault has Martius in small degree*
23 topping: *surpassing*

how you are censured here in the city, I mean
of us o' the right-hand file? Do you?

Both. Why, how are we censured?

Men. Because you talk of pride now,—Will 28
you not be angry?

Both. Well, well, sir; well.

Men. Why, 'tis no great matter; for a very
little thief of occasion will rob you of a great 32
deal of patience: give your dispositions the
reins, and be angry at your pleasures; at the
least, if you take it as a pleasure to you in
being so. You blame Martius for being proud? 36

Bru. We do it not alone, sir.

Men. I know you can do very little alone;
for your helps are many, or else your actions
would grow wondrous single: your abilities are 40
too infant-like for doing much alone. You talk
of pride: O that you could turn your eyes
towards the napes of your necks, and make but
an interior survey of your good selves! O that 44
you could!

Both. What then, sir?

Men. Why, then you should discover a brace
of unmeriting, proud, violent, testy magis- 18
trates—alias fools—as any in Rome.

Sic. Menenius, you are known well enough
too.

Men. I am known to be a humorous patri- 52
cian, and one that loves a cup of hot wine with
not a drop of allaying Tiber in 't; said to be

25 censured: *estimated*
26 right-hand file: *conservative, aristocratic party*
31, 32 a very . . . occasion: *a very little occasion, acting like a thief*
40 single: *simple, weak*   42-44 O that . . . good selves; *cf. n.*
52 humorous: *whimsical*
54 allaying Tiber: *diluting water; cf. n.*

something imperfect in favouring the first complaint; hasty and tinder-like upon too trivial 56
motion; one that converses more with the buttock of the night than with the forehead of the
morning. What I think I utter, and spend my
malice in my breath. Meeting two such weals- 60
men as you are,—I cannot call you Lycurguses,
—if the drink you give me touch my palate
adversely, I make a crooked face at it. I cannot
say your worships have delivered the matter 64
well when I find the ass in compound with the
major part of your syllables; and though I
must be content to bear with those that say you
are reverend grave men, yet they lie deadly that 68
tell you have good faces. If you see this in the
map of my microcosm, follows it that I am
known well enough too? What harm can your
bisson conspectuities glean out of this character, 72
if I be known well enough too?

Bru. Come, sir, come, we know you well
enough.

Men. You know neither me, yourselves, nor 76
anything. You are ambitious for poor knaves'
caps and legs: you wear out a good wholesome
forenoon in hearing a cause between an orange-
wife and a fosset-seller, and then rejourn the 80
controversy of three-pence to a second day of

55 something . . . complaint: *somewhat hasty in judgment*
57 motion: *occasion, incitement*   57-59 one . . . morning; *cf. n.*
59, 60 spend . . . breath: *get rid of my ill will by putting it into
words*   60 wealsmen: *politicians*
61 Lycurguses: *great lawgivers*
63-66 I cannot . . . syllables; *cf. n.*
70 map . . . microcosm; *cf. n.*
72 bisson conspectuities: *blinded sight; cf. n.*
78 caps and legs: *applause and reverence*
79 orange-wife: *hawker of oranges*
80 fosset-seller: *seller of faucets, taps for barrels*   rejourn: *post-
pone*

audience. When you are hearing a matter between party and party, if you chance to be
pinched with the colic, you make faces like 84
mummers, set up the bloody flag against all
patience, and, in roaring for a chamber-pot, dismiss the controversy bleeding, the more en-
tangled by your hearing: all the peace you make 88
in their cause is, calling both the parties knaves.
You are a pair of strange ones.

Bru. Come, come, you are well understood
to be a perfecter giber for the table than a 92
necessary bencher in the Capitol.

Men. Our very priests must become mockers
if they shall encounter such ridiculous subjects
as you are. When you speak best unto the 96
purpose it is not worth the wagging of your
beards; and your beards deserve not so honourable a grave as to stuff a botcher's cushion, or
to be entombed in an ass's pack-saddle. Yet you 100
must be saying Martius is proud; who, in a
cheap estimation, is worth all your predecessors
since Deucalion, though peradventure some of
the best of 'em were hereditary hangmen. Good 104
den to your worships: more of your conversation would infect my brain, being the herdsmen
of the beastly plebeians: I will be bold to take
my leave of you.   108

Brutus and Sicinius [go] aside.

Enter Volumnia, Virgilia, and Valeria.

---

85 mummers: *rustic actors*   set . . . flag: *proclaim violent war*
91-93 *Cf. n.*
97, 98 not worth . . .   beards: *not worth the effort of opening and*
    closing your mouths   99 botcher's: *patching tailor's*
102 estimation: *valuation*   103 Deucalion: *the Greek Noah*
104, 105 Good den: *good evening*

How now, my as fair as noble ladies,—and the
moon, were she earthly, no nobler,—whither
do you follow your eyes so fast?

Vol. Honourable Menenius, my boy Martius 112
approaches; for the love of Juno, let's go.

Men. Ha! Martius coming home?

Vol. Ay, worthy Menenius; and with most
prosperous approbation.   116

Men. Take my cap, Jupiter, and I thank
thee. Hoo! Martius coming home!

2 Ladies. Nay, 'tis true.

Vol. Look, here's a letter from him: the 120
state hath another, his wife another; and, I
think, there's one at home for you.

Men. I will make my very house reel to-
night. A letter for me!   124

Vir. Yes, certain, there's a letter for you; I
saw 't.

Men. A letter for me! It gives me an estate
of seven years' health; in which time I will 128
make a lip at the physician: the most sovereign
prescription in Galen is but empiricutic, and, to
this preservative, of no better report than a
horse-drench. Is he not wounded? he was wont 132
to come home wounded.

Vir. O! no, no, no.

Vol. O! he is wounded, I thank the gods for 't.

Men. So do I too, if it be not too much. 136
Brings a' victory in his pocket? The wounds
become him.

111 your eyes: *the eager looks you caſt ahead*
116 prosperous approbation: *positive success*
117 Take . . . Jupiter: *i.e. I throw my cap high in the air*
129 make a lip at: *defy*   sovereign: *efficacious*
130 empiricutic: *experimental, quackish*   to: *in comparison with*

Vol. On's brows, Menenius; he comes the third time home with the oaken garland.   140

Men. Has he disciplined Aufidius soundly?

Vol. Titus Lartius writes they fought together, but Aufidius got off.

Men. And 'twas time for him too, I'll war- 144 rant him that: an he had stayed by him I would not have been so fidiused for all the chests in Corioli, and the gold that's in them. Is the senate possessed of this?   148

Vol. Good ladies, let's go. Yes, yes, yes; the senate has letters from the general, wherein he gives my son the whole name of the war. He hath in this action outdone his former deeds 152 doubly.

Val. In troth there's wondrous things spoke of him.

Men. Wondrous! ay, I warrant you, and not 156 without his true purchasing.

Vir. The gods grant them true!

Vol. True! pow, wow.

Men. True! I'll be sworn they are true. 160 Where is he wounded? [*To the Tribunes.*] God save your good worships! Martius is coming home: he has more cause to be proud. [*To Volumnia.*] Where is he wounded?   164

Vol. I' the shoulder, and i' the left arm: there will be large cicatrices to show the people when he shall stand for his place. He received in the repulse of Tarquin seven hurts i' the body.   168

---

139 On 's brows: *i.e. not in his pocket*
146 fidiused: *Aufidiused, put in Aufidius' proper place*
148 possessed: *informed*   151 name: *reputation*
167 stand . . . place: *seek the consulship*
168 repulse of Tarquin; *cf. n.*

Men. One i' the neck, and two i' the thigh, there's nine that I know.

Vol. He had, before this last expedition, twenty-five wounds upon him.   172

Men. Now, it's twenty-seven: every gash was an enemy's grave.

Hark! the trumpets.   *A shout and flourish.*

Vol. These are the ushers of Martius: before 176 him he carries noise, and behind him he leaves tears:

Death, that dark spirit, in 's nervy arm doth lie;

Which, being advanc'd, declines, and then men die. 180

A Sennet. Trumpets sound. Enter Cominius, the General, and Titus Lartius; between them, Coriolanus, crowned with an oaken garland; with Captains and Soldiers, and a Herald.

Her. Know, Rome, that all alone Martius did fight

Within Corioli gates: where he hath won,

With fame, a name to Caius Martius; these

In honour follows Coriolanus.   184

Welcome to Rome, renowned Coriolanus!

                        Sound. Flourish.

All. Welcome to Rome, renowned Coriolanus!

Cor. No more of this; it does offend my heart:

Pray now, no more.

Com.   Look, sir, your mother!

Cor.   O! 188

You have, I know, petition'd all the gods

For my prosperity.   *Kneels.*

Vol.   Nay, my good soldier, up;

My gentle Martius, worthy Caius, and

170 nine; cf. n.   179 nervy: *muscular*
180 advanc'd: *raised*   declines: *falls*
180 S. d. Sennet: *trumpet signal for a procession to move*
183 to: *added to*

By deed-achieving honour newly nam'd,—   192
What is it?—Coriolanus must I call thee?
But O! thy wife!—

   Cor.   My gracious silence, hail!
Wouldst thou have laugh'd had I come coffin'd home,
That weep'st to see me triumph? Ah! my dear,   196
Such eyes the widows in Corioli wear,
And mothers that lack sons.

   Men.   Now, the gods crown thee!

   Cor. And live you yet? [*To Valeria.*] O my sweet
      lady, pardon.   199

   Vol. I know not where to turn: O! welcome home;
And welcome, general; and y' are welcome all.

   Men. A hundred thousand welcomes: I could weep,
And I could laugh; I am light, and heavy. Welcome.
A curse begin at very root on 's heart   204
That is not glad to see thee! You are three
That Rome should dote on; yet, by the faith of men,
We have some old crab-trees here at home that will not
Be grafted to your relish. Yet, welcome, warriors! 208
We call a nettle but a nettle, and
The faults of fools but folly.

   Com.   Ever right.

   Cor. Menenius, ever, ever.

   Her. Give way there, and go on!

   Cor. [*To Volumnia and Virgilia.*] Your hand, and
      yours: 212
Ere in our own house I do shade my head,
The good patricians must be visited;
From whom I have receiv'd not only greetings,

---

194 My gracious silence; *cf. n.*
200 I . . . turn; *cf. n.*   204 begin; *cf. n.*
207 crab-trees: *crabapple trees, i.e. the sour tribunes*
208 Be . . . relish: *be brought to taste like you*
211 Menenius . . . ever: *still the same Menenius*

But with them change of honours.

Vol.   I have liv'd   216
To see inherited my very wishes,
And the buildings of my fancy: only
There's one thing wanting, which I doubt not but
Our Rome will cast upon thee.

Cor.   Know, good mother, 220
I had rather be their servant in my way
Than sway with them in theirs.

Com. On, to the Capitol!

> *Flourish. Cornets. Exeunt in state, as before.*

> *Enter Brutus and Sicinius.*

Bru. All tongues speak of him, and the bleared
     sights   224
Are spectacled to see him: your prattling nurse
Into a rapture lets her baby cry
While she chats him: the kitchen malkin pins
Her richest lockram 'bout her reechy neck,   228
Clambering the walls to eye him: stalls, bulks, win-
     dows
Are smother'd up, leads fill'd, and ridges hors'd
With variable complexions, all agreeing
In earnestness to see him: seld-shown flamens   232
Do press among the popular throngs, and puff
To win a vulgar station; our veil'd dames
Commit the war of white and damask in

216 change: *a variety*
217 inherited: *realized, come into my possession*
222 sway with: *rule*   223 S. d. Enter, etc.; *cf. n.*
226 rapture: *fit*   227 chats: *gossips about*   malkin: *wench*
228 lockram: *linen cloth*   reechy: *dirty*
229 bulks: *projecting shelves outside a shop*
230 leads: *lead-covered roofs*   ridges hors'd: *roof tops bestridden*
231 variable complexions: *all types of people*
232 seld-shown flamens: *priests who seldom show themselves*
233 popular throngs: *crowds of rabble*
234 vulgar station: *place in the mob*

Their nicely-gawded cheeks to the wanton spoil   236
Of Phœbus' burning kisses: such a pother
As if that whatsoever god who leads him
Were slily crept into his human powers,
And gave him graceful posture.
    Sic.   On the sudden 240
I warrant him consul.
    Bru.   Then our office may,
During his power, go sleep.
    Sic. He cannot temperately transport his honours
From where he should begin and end, but will   244
Lose those he hath won.
    Bru.   In that there's comfort.
    Sic. Doubt not the commoners, for whom we stand,
But they upon their ancient malice will
Forget with the least cause these his new honours, 248
Which that he'll give them, make I as little question
As he is proud to do 't.
    Bru.   I heard him swear,
Were he to stand for consul, never would he
Appear i' the market-place, nor on him put   252
The napless vesture of humility;
Nor, showing, as the manner is, his wounds
To the people, beg their stinking breaths.
    Sic.   'Tis right.
    Bru. It was his word. O! he would miss it rather 256
Than carry it but by the suit of the gentry to him
And the desire of the nobles.
    Sic.   I wish no better
Than have him hold that purpose and to put it
In execution.
    Bru.   'Tis most like he will.   260

236 nicely-gawded: *daintily colored*   237 pother: *hubbub*
243, 244 He . . . end; *cf. n.*   247 upon: *on account of*
253 napless: *threadbare*   257 but: *otherwise than*

Sic. It shall be to him then, as our good wills,
A sure destruction.

Bru.   So it must fall out
To him or our authorities. For an end,
We must suggest the people in what hatred   264
He still hath held them; that to 's power he would
Have made them mules, silenc'd their pleaders, and
Dispropertied their freedoms; holding them,
In human action and capacity,   268
Of no more soul nor fitness for the world
Than camels in their war; who have their provand
Only for bearing burthens, and sore blows
For sinking under them.

Sic.   This, as you say, suggested 272
At some time when his soaring insolence
Shall teach the people—which time shall not want,
If he be put upon 't; and that's as easy
As to set dogs on sheep—will be his fire   276
To kindle their dry stubble; and their blaze
Shall darken him for ever.

Enter a Messenger.

Bru.   What's the matter?
Mess. You are sent for to the Capitol. 'Tis thought
That Martius shall be consul.   280
I have seen the dumb men throng to see him, and
The blind to hear him speak: matrons flung gloves,
Ladies and maids their scarfs and handkerchers
Upon him as he pass'd; the nobles bended,   284
As to Jove's statue, and the commons made

261 as . . . wills: *as we would have it*   263 For an end: *in short*
264 suggest: *remind by insinuation*   265 still: *always*
266 mules: *beasts of burden*   267 Dispropertied: *annulled*
270 provand: *food*   274 teach; *cf. n.*
275 put upon 't: *provoked*
276 will . . . fire: *will be in him like a spark*
278 darken: *tarnish, remove the gloss from*

A shower and thunder with their caps and shouts:
I never saw the like.
  Bru.   Let's to the Capitol;
And carry with us ears and eyes for the time,   288
But hearts for the event.
  Sic.   Have with you.   *Exeunt.*

Scene Two

[*The Same.   The Capitol*]

Enter two Officers to lay cushions, as it were, in the Capitol.

  1. Off. Come, come, they are almost here.
How many stand for consulships?

  2. Off. Three, they say; but 'tis thought of
every one Coriolanus will carry it.   4

  1. Off. That's a brave fellow; but he's
vengeance proud, and loves not the common
people.

  2. Off. Faith, there hath been many great 8
men that have flattered the people, who ne'er
loved them; and there be many that they have
loved, they know not wherefore: so that if they
love they know not why, they hate upon no 12
better a ground. Therefore, for Coriolanus
neither to care whether they love or hate him
manifests the true knowledge he has in their
disposition; and out of his noble carelessness lets 16
them plainly see 't.

  1. Off. If he did not care whether he had

---

286 shower: *i.e. of falling caps*   288 time: *the present spectacle*
289 hearts . . . event: *i.e. keep our minds intent upon what is to fol-
    low*   Have with you: *let us go*   4 carry: *win*
6 vengeance: *accursedly*   9 who: *i.e. the people*
15 in: *concerning*

their love or no, he waved indifferently 'twixt
doing them neither good nor harm; but he seeks 20
their hate with greater devotion than they can
render it him; and leaves nothing undone that
may fully discover him their opposite. Now, to
seem to affect the malice and displeasure of the 24
people is as bad as that which he dislikes, to
flatter them for their love.

2. Off. He hath deserved worthily of his
country; and his ascent is not by such easy 28
degrees as those who, having been supple and
courteous to the people, bonneted, without any
further deed to have them at all into their
estimation and report; but he hath so planted 32
his honours in their eyes, and his actions in
their hearts, that for their tongues to be silent,
and not confess so much, were a kind of ingrateful injury; to report otherwise were a 36
malice, that, giving itself the lie, would pluck
reproof and rebuke from every ear that heard
it.

1. Off. No more of him; he's a worthy man: 40
make way, they are coming.

*A Sennet. Enter the Patricians, and the Tribunes of
the People, Lictors before them: Coriolanus, Menenius, Cominius the Consul. Sicinius and Brutus take
their places by themselves: Coriolanus stands.*

Men. Having determin'd of the Volsces, and
To send for Titus Lartius, it remains, 42

---

19 waved indifferently: *would waver impartially*
21 devotion: *earnestness*
23 discover: *manifest*   opposite: *adversary*
24 affect: *aim at, desire*   28, 29 easy degrees: *gradual steps*
30 bonneted: *with hats off*
37 giving . . . lie: *manifesting its own falsehood*
42 determin'd of: *reached a decision concerning*

As the main point of this our after-meeting,   44
To gratify his noble service that
Hath thus stood for his country: therefore, please you,
Most reverend and grave elders, to desire
The present consul, and last general   48
In our well-found successes, to report
A little of that worthy work perform'd
By Caius Martius Coriolanus, whom
We meet here both to thank and to remember   52
With honours like himself.

 1. Sen.   Speak, good Cominius:
Leave nothing out for length, and make us think
Rather our state's defective for requital,
Than we to stretch it out. [*To the Tribunes.*] Masters
 o' the people,   56
We do request your kindest ears, and, after,
Your loving motion toward the common body,
To yield what passes here.

 Sic.   We are convented
Upon a pleasing treaty, and have hearts   60
Inclinable to honour and advance
The theme of our assembly.

 Bru.   Which the rather
We shall be bless'd to do, if he remember
A kinder value of the people than   64
He hath hereto priz'd them at.

 Men.   That's off, that's off;
I would you rather had been silent.   Please you
To hear Cominius speak?

---

45 gratify: *reward*   46 stood for: *supported*
49 well-found: *auspicious*   53 like himself: *worthy of him*
55 defective: *insufficient*
56 Than . . . out: *than we deficient in seeking to make the largest re-*
 quital   58 motion toward: *proposal to*
59 passes: *is voted*   convented: *called together*
60 treaty: *proposal*   62 theme: *subject, i.e. Coriolanus*
63 bless'd: *happy*   64 kinder value: *more favorable opinion*
65 off: *amiss*

Bru.   Most willingly;
But yet my caution was more pertinent   68
Than the rebuke you give it.
  Men.   He loves your people;
But tie him not to be their bedfellow.
Worthy Cominius, speak.
                    Coriolanus rises, and offers to go away.
                              Nay, keep your place.
  Sen. Sit, Coriolanus; never shame to hear   72
What you have nobly done.
  Cor.   Your honours' pardon:
I had rather have my wounds to heal again
Than hear say how I got them.
  Bru.   Sir, I hope
My words disbench'd you not.
  Cor.   No, sir: yet oft,   76
When blows have made me stay, I fled from words.
You sooth'd not, therefore hurt not. But your people,
I love them as they weigh—
  Men.   Pray now, sit down.
  Cor. I had rather have one scratch my head i' the
      sun   80
When the alarum were struck than idly sit
To hear my nothings monster'd.   *Exit Coriolanus.*
  Men.   Masters of the people,
Your multiplying spawn how can he flatter,—
That's thousand to one good one,—when you now
      see   84
He had rather venture all his limbs for honour
Than one on 's ears to hear it? Proceed, Cominius.
  Com. I shall lack voice: the deeds of Coriolanus

76 disbench'd: *unseated*   78 sooth'd: *flattered*
79 as they weigh: *according to their worth*
82 monster'd: *grotesquely exaggerated*
84 That's . . . good one: *of whom only one in a thousand is good*

Should not be utter'd feebly. It is held   88
That valour is the chiefest virtue, and
Most dignifies the haver: if it be,
The man I speak of cannot in the world
Be singly counterpois'd.   At sixteen years,   92
When Tarquin made a head for Rome, he fought
Beyond the mark of others; our then dictator,
Whom with all praise I point at, saw him fight,
When with his Amazonian chin he drove   96
The bristled lips before him. He bestrid
An o'er-press'd Roman, and i' the consul's view
Slew three opposers: Tarquin's self he met,
And struck him on his knee: in that day's feats,   100
When he might act the woman in the scene,
He prov'd best man i' the field, and for his meed
Was brow-bound with the oak. His pupil age
Man-enter'd thus, he waxed like a sea, *natural force*   104
And in the brunt of seventeen battles since
He lurch'd all swords of the garland. For this last,
Before and in Corioli, let me say,
I cannot speak him home: he stopp'd the fliers,   108
And by his rare example made the coward
Turn terror into sport: as weeds before
A vessel under sail, so men obey'd,
And fell below his stem: his sword, death's stamp,   112
Where it did mark, it took; from face to foot
He was a thing of blood, whose every motion

90 haver: *possessor*
92 Be . . . counterpois'd: *find any single equal*
93 made . . . for: *raised an army against*
94 mark; *cf. n.*   96 Amazonian: *i.e. beardless*
100 on his knee: *with such force as to bring him to his knee*
101 in the scene: *on the stage*
104 Man-enter'd: *entered upon manhood*
106 lurch'd: *robbed; cf. n.*
108 speak him home: *do him full justice*
112 fell . . . stem: *yielded to his course*
113 took: *took possession, slew*

Was tim'd with dying cries: alone he enter'd
The mortal gate of the city, which he painted   116
With shunless destiny; aidless came off,
And with a sudden re-enforcement struck
Corioli like a planet.   Now all's his:
When by and by the din of war 'gan pierce   120
His ready sense; then straight his doubled spirit
Re-quicken'd what in flesh was fatigate,
And to the battle came he; where he did
Run reeking o'er the lives of men, as if   124
'Twere a perpetual spoil; and till we call'd
Both field and city ours, he never stood
To ease his breast with panting.
  Men.   Worthy man!
  Sen. He cannot but with measure fit the honours 128
Which we devise him.
  Com.   Our spoils he kick'd at,
And look'd upon things precious as they were
The common muck o' the world: he covets less
Than misery itself would give; rewards   132
His deeds with doing them, and is content
To spend the time to end it.
  Men.   He's right noble:
Let him be call'd for.
  Sen.   Call Coriolanus.
  Off. He doth appear.   136

Enter Coriolanus.

  Men. The senate, Coriolanus, are well pleas'd
To make thee consul.
  Cor.   I do owe them still
My life and services.

116, 117 painted . . . destiny: *stained with the blood of those who
 could not escape their doom*   120 by and by: *immediately*
122 fatigate: *wearied*   129 kick'd at: *scorned*
130 as: *as if*   134 to end it: *merely to kill time*

 Men.   It then remains
That you do speak to the people.
 Cor.   I do beseech you, 140
Let me o'erleap that custom, for I cannot
Put on the gown, stand naked, and entreat them,
For my wounds' sake, to give their suffrage: please
  you,
That I may pass this doing.
 Sic.   Sir, the people 144
Must have their voices; neither will they bate
One jot of ceremony.
 Men.   Put them not to 't:
Pray you, go fit you to the custom, and
Take to you, as your predecessors have, 148
Your honour with your form.
 Cor.   It is a part
That I shall blush in acting, and might well
Be taken from the people.
 Bru. [*Aside to Sicinius.*] Mark you that?
 Cor. To brag unto them, thus I did, and thus; 152
Show them the unaching scars which I should hide,
As if I had receiv'd them for the hire
Of their breath only!
 Men.   Do not stand upon 't.
We recommend to you, tribunes of the people, 156
Our purpose to them; and to our noble consul
Wish we all joy and honour.
 Sen. To Coriolanus come all joy and honour!
      Flourish Cornets. Then exeunt.
      Mane[n]t Sicinius and Brutus.

144 pass this doing: *omit this action*
145 voices: *votes* bate: *abate, waive*
146 Put . . . to 't: *do not force the issue*
147 fit you: *accommodate yourself*
149 with your form: *in the conventional manner*
155 breath: *i.e. votes*   156 recommend: *entrust*
157 Our . . . them: *what we propose to them*

Bru. You see how he intends to use the people.   160

Sic. May they perceive 's intent! He will **require** them,

As if he did contemn what he requested

Should be in them to give.

Bru.   Come; we'll inform them

Of our proceedings here: on the market-place   164

I know they do attend us.   [*Exeunt.*]

Scene Three

[*The Same.   The Forum*]

Enter seven or eight Citizens.

1. Cit. Once, if he do require our voices, we ought not to deny him.

2. Cit. We may, sir, if we will.

3. Cit. We have power in ourselves to do 4 it, but it is a power that we have no power to do; for if he show us his wounds, and tell us his deeds, we are to put our tongues into those wounds and speak for them; so, if he tell us his 8 noble deeds, we must also tell him our noble acceptance of them. Ingratitude is monstrous, and for the multitude to be ingrateful were to make a monster of the multitude; of the which 12 we being members, should bring ourselves to be monstrous members.

1. Cit. And to make us no better thought of, a little help will serve; for once we stood up about 16 the corn, he himself stuck not to call us the many-headed multitude.

161 require: *request*

1 Once: *once for all*

17 stuck: *hesitated*

162 contemn what: *scorn that what*

16 once: *once when*

3. Cit. We have been called so of many; not
that our heads are some brown, some black, some 20
abram, some bald, but that our wits are so di-
versely coloured: and truly I think, if all our
wits were to issue out of one skull, they would
fly east, west, north, south; and their consent of 24
one direct way should be at once to all the points
o' the compass.

2. Cit. Think you so? Which way do you judge
my wit would fly?   28

3. Cit. Nay, your wit will not so soon out as
another man's will; 'tis strongly wedged up in
a block-head; but if it were at liberty, 'twould,
sure, southward.   32

2. Cit. Why that way?

3. Cit. To lose itself in a fog; where being
three parts melted away with rotten dews, the
fourth would return for conscience' sake, to help 36
to get thee a wife.

2. Cit. You are never without your tricks: you
may, you may.

3. Cit. Are you all resolved to give your voices? 40
But that's no matter, the greater part carries it.
I say, if he would incline to the people, there
was never a worthier man.

*Enter Coriolanus, in a gown of humility, with
Menenius.*

Here he comes, and in the gown of humility: 44
mark his behaviour. We are not to stay all
together, but to come by him where he stands,
by ones, by twos, and by threes. He's to make

---

21 abram: *auburn*   24 consent of: *agreement about*
35 rotten dews: *infectious vapors*
39 you may: *you may have your joke*   41 greater part: *majority*

his requests by particulars; wherein every one 48
of us has a single honour, in giving him our own
voices with our own tongues: therefore follow
me, and I'll direct you how you shall go by him.

 All. Content, content.   [*Exeunt Citizens.*] 52

 Men. O, sir, you are not right: have you not known
The worthiest men have done 't?

 Cor.   What must I say?
'I pray, sir,'—Plague upon 't! I cannot bring
My tongue to such a pace. 'Look, sir, my wounds! 56
I got them in my country's service, when
Some certain of your brethren roar'd and ran
From the noise of our own drums.'

 Men.   O me! the gods!
You must not speak of that: you must desire them 60
To think upon you.

 Cor.   Think upon me! Hang 'em!
I would they would forget me, like the virtues
Which our divines lose by 'em.

 Men.   You'll mar all:
I'll leave you. Pray you, speak to 'em, I pray you, 64
In wholesome manner.   *Exit.*

Enter two of the Citizens.

 Cor.   Bid them wash their faces,
And keep their teeth clean. So, here comes a brace.
You know the cause, sir, of my standing here?

 1. Cit. We do, sir; tell us what hath brought 68
you to 't.

 Cor. Mine own desert.

 2. Cit. Your own desert!

---

48 by particulars: *individually*   49 single: *separate*
63 lose by 'em: *i.e. vainly seek to propagate in them by preaching*
65 wholesome: *sane, reasonable*   65 S. d. two of the Citizens; *cf. n.*

Cor. Ay, not mine own desire.   72

1. Cit. How! not your own desire?

Cor. No, sir, 'twas never my desire yet to trouble the poor with begging.

1. Cit. You must think, if we give you anything, 76 we hope to gain by you.

Cor. Well, then, I pray, your price o' the consulship?

1. Cit. The price is, to ask it kindly.   80

Cor. Kindly! sir, I pray, let me ha 't: I have wounds to show you, which shall be yours in private. Your good voice, sir; what say you?

2. Cit. You shall ha 't, worthy sir.   84

Cor. A match, sir. There's in all two worthy voices begged. I have your alms: adieu.

1. Cit. But this is something odd.

2. Cit. An 'twere to give again,—but 'tis no 88 matter.   *Exeunt.*

Enter two other Citizens.

Cor. Pray you now, if it may stand with the tune of your voices that I may be consul, I have here the customary gown.   92

1. Cit. You have deserved nobly of your country, and you have not deserved nobly.

Cor. Your enigma?

1. Cit. You have been a scourge to her enemies, 96 you have been a rod to her friends; you have not indeed loved the common people.

Cor. You should account me the more virtuous that I have not been common in my love. 100 I will, sir, flatter my sworn brother the people, to earn a dearer estimation of them; 'tis a condition they account gentle: and since the wis-

dom of their choice is rather to have my hat 104
than my heart, I will practise the insinuating
nod, and be off to them most counterfeitly; that
is, sir, I will counterfeit the bewitchment of
some popular man, and give it bountiful to 108
the desirers. Therefore, beseech you, I may be
consul.

2. Cit. We hope to find you our friend, and
therefore give you our voices heartily. 112

1. Cit. You have received many wounds for
your country.

Cor. I will not seal your knowledge with
showing them. I will make much of your voices, 116
and so trouble you no farther.

Both. The gods give you joy, sir, heartily!

[*Exeunt.*]

Cor. Most sweet voices!
Better it is to die, better to starve, 120
Than crave the hire which first we do deserve.
Why in this wolfish toge should I stand here,
To beg of Hob and Dick, that does appear,
Their needless vouches? Custom calls me to 't: 124
What custom wills, in all things should we do 't,
The dust on antique time would lie unswept,
And mountainous error be too highly heap'd
For truth to o'er-peer. Rather than fool it so, 128
Let the high office and the honour go
To one that would do thus. I am half through;
The one part suffer'd, the other will I do.

---

106 be off: *bare my head*   counterfeitly: *hypocritically*
107 bewitchment: *sorcery*
108 popular man: *demagogue*   bountiful: *bountifully*
115 seal: *confirm*   121 first: *previously, already*
122 wolfish toge; *cf. n.*
123 Hob . . . appear: *whatever plebeian appears*
124 needless vouches: *unnecessary confirmations*
128 o'er-peer: *peep over the accumulation of tradition*   fool it:
     play the fool

Enter three Citizens more.

Here come moe voices.   132
Your voices: for your voices I have fought;
Watch'd for your voices; for your voices bear
Of wounds two dozen odd; battles thrice six
I have seen and heard of; for your voices have   136
Done many things, some less, some more; your voices:
Indeed, I would be consul.
    1. Cit. He has done nobly, and cannot go with-
out any honest man's voice.   140
    2. Cit. Therefore let him be consul.   The gods
give him joy, and make him good friend to the
people!
    All. Amen, amen.   144
God save thee, noble consul!   [*Exeunt Citizens.*]
    Cor.   Worthy voices!

Enter Menenius, with Brutus and Sicinius.

    Men. You have stood your limitation; and the trib-
      unes
Endue you with the people's voice: remains
That, in th' official marks invested, you   148
Anon do meet the senate.
    Cor.   Is this done?
    Sic. The custom of request you have discharg'd:
The people do admit you, and are summon'd
To meet anon, upon your approbation.   152
    Cor. Where? at the senate-house?
    Sic.   There, Coriolanus.
    Cor. May I change these garments?
    Sic. You may, sir.

134 Watch'd: *done vigil*   146 limitation: *fixed period of time*
147 remains: *it remains*   148 marks: *emblems of authority*
152 upon: *on the business of*

Cor. That I'll straight do; and, knowing myself
again,   156
Repair to the senate-house.

Men. I'll keep you company.   Will you along?

Bru. We stay here for the people.

Sic.   Fare you well.

     Exeunt Coriolanus and Menenius.

He has it now; and by his looks, methinks,   160
'Tis warm at 's heart.

Bru.   With a proud heart he wore
His humble weeds.   Will you dismiss the people?

Enter the Plebeians.

Sic. How now, my masters! have you chose this
 man?

1. Cit. He has our voices, sir.   164

Bru. We pray the gods he may deserve your loves.

2. Cit. Amen, sir.   To my poor unworthy notice,
He mock'd us when he begg'd our voices.

3. Cit.   Certainly,
He flouted us downright.   168

1. Cit. No, 'tis his kind of speech; he did not mock
 us.

2. Cit. Not one amongst us, save yourself, but says
He us'd us scornfully: he should have show'd us
His marks of merit, wounds receiv'd for 's country. 172

Sic. Why, so he did, I am sure.

All.   No, no; no man saw 'em.

3. Cit. He said he had wounds, which he could show
 in private;
And with his hat, thus waving it in scorn,
'I would be consul,' says he: 'aged custom,   176
But by your voices, will not so permit me;

161 'Tis . . . heart: *it warms his heart*

Your voices therefore': when we granted that,
Here was, 'I thank you for your voices, thank you,
Your most sweet voices: now you have left your
    voices, 180
I have no further with you.' Was not this mockery?
  Sic. Why either were you ignorant to see 't,
Or, seeing it, of such childish friendliness
To yield your voices?
    Bru.   Could you not have told him 184
As you were lesson'd, when he had no power,
But was a petty servant to the state,
He was your enemy, ever spake against
Your liberties and the charters that you bear 188
I' the body of the weal; and now, arriving
A place of potency and sway o' the state,
If he should still malignantly remain
Fast foe to the plebeii, your voices might 192
Be curses to yourselves? You should have said
That as his worthy deeds did claim no less
Than what he stood for, so his gracious nature
Would think upon you for your voices and 196
Translate his malice towards you into love,
Standing your friendly lord.
    Sic.   Thus to have said,
As you were fore-advis'd, had touch'd his spirit
And tried his inclination; from him pluck'd 200
Either his gracious promise, which you might,
As cause had call'd you up, have held him to;
Or else it would have gall'd his surly nature,
Which easily endures not article 204
Tying him to aught; so, putting him to rage,

182 ignorant to: *so dull as not to*   185 lesson'd: *instructed*
188 charters: *privileges*
189 weal: *commonwealth*   arriving: *attaining*
202 call'd you up: *summoned you*   204 article: *condition*

You should have ta'en th' advantage of his choler,
And pass'd•him unelected.

   Bru.   Did you perceive
He did solicit you in free contempt   208
When he did need your loves, and do you think
That his contempt shall not be bruising to you
When he hath power to crush? Why, had your bodies
No heart among you? or had you tongues to cry   212
Against the rectorship of judgment?

   Sic.   Have you
Ere now denied the asker? and now again
Of him that did not ask, but mock, bestow
Your su'd-for tongues?   216

   3. Cit. He's not confirm'd; we may deny him yet.

   2. Cit. And will deny him:
I'll have five hundred voices of that sound.

   1. Cit. Ay, twice five hundred and their friends to
      piece 'em.   220

   Bru. Get you hence instantly, and tell those friends,
They have chose a consul that will from them take
Their liberties; make them of no more voice
Than dogs that are as often beat for barking   224
As therefore kept to do so.

   Sic.   Let them assemble;
And, on a safer judgment, all revoke
Your ignorant election. Enforce his pride,
And his old hate unto you; besides, forget not   228
With what contempt he wore the humble weed;
How in his suit he scorn'd you; but your loves,
Thinking upon his services, took from you
The apprehension of his present portance,   232

213 rectorship: *guiding power*   215 Of: *upon*
220 piece: *reinforce*   226 safer: *more prudent*
227 Enforce: *lay stress upon*
232 apprehension: *discernment*   portance: *behavior*

Which most gibingly, ungravely, he did fashion
After the inveterate hate he bears you.
  Bru.   Lay
A fault on us, your tribunes; that we labour'd,—
No impediment between,—but that you must   236
Cast your election on him.
  Sic.   Say, you chose him
More after our commandment than as guided
By your own true affections; and that, your minds,
Pre-occupied with what you rather must do   240
Than what you should, made you against the grain
To voice him consul: lay the fault on us.
  Bru. Ay, spare us not. Say we read lectures to you,
How youngly he began to serve his country, 244
How long continu'd, and what stock he springs of,
The noble house o' the Martians, from whence came
That Ancus Martius, Numa's daughter's son,
Who, after great Hostilius, here was king;   248
Of the same house Publius and Quintus were,
That our best water brought by conduits hither;
And Censorinus, that was so surnam'd,—
And nobly nam'd so, twice being censor,—   252
Was his great ancestor.
  Sic.   One thus descended,
That hath, beside, well in his person wrought
To be set high in place, we did commend
To your remembrances: but you have found,   256
Scaling his present bearing with his past,
That he's your fixed enemy, and revoke
Your sudden approbation.
  Bru.   Say you ne'er had done 't—
Harp on that still—but by our putting on;   260

234 After: *in accord with·*
236 No . . . between: *without admitting any impediment*
251 *Cf. n.*   257 Scaling: *balancing*   260 putting on: *urging*

And presently, when you have drawn your number,
Repair to the Capitol.

  All.   We will so; almost all
Repent in their election.   *Exeunt Plebeians.*

  Bru.   Let them go on;
This mutiny were better put in hazard   264
Than stay, past doubt, for greater.
If, as his nature is, he fall in rage
With their refusal, both observe and answer
The vantage of his anger.

  Sic.   To the Capitol, come: 268
We will be there before the stream o' the people;
And this shall seem, as partly 'tis, their own,
Which we have goaded onward.   *Exeunt.*

ACT THIRD

Scene One

[*Rome. A Street*]

*Cornets. Enter Coriolanus, Menenius, all the Gentry,
Cominius, Titus Lartius, and other Senators.*

  Cor. Tullus Aufidius then had made new head?

  Lart. He had, my lord; and that it was which caus'd
Our swifter composition.

  Cor. So then the Volsces stand but as at first, 4
Ready, when time shall prompt them, to make road
Upon 's again.

  Com.   They are worn, lord consul, so,

---

261 drawn . . . number: *collected a sufficient number*
263 Repent in: *repent of*   264 put in hazard: *risked*
265 stay . . . greater: *that we should wait for a greater, inevitable
  hazard*   267, 268 answer . . . vantage: *make use*
1 made new head: *raised a new army*
3 composition: *coming to terms*   5 road: *an inroad, raid*

That we shall hardly in our ages see
Their banners wave again.

    Cor.   Saw you Aufidius?   8

    Lart. On safeguard he came to me; and did curse
Against the Volsces, for they had so vilely
Yielded the town: he is retir'd to Antium.

    Cor. Spoke he of me?

    Lart.   He did, my lord.

    Cor.   How? what? 12

    Lart. How often he had met you, sword to sword;
That of all things upon the earth he hated
Your person most; that he would pawn his fortunes
To hopeless restitution, so he might   16
Be call'd your vanquisher.

    Cor.   At Antium lives he?

    Lart. At Antium.

    Cor. I wish I had a cause to seek him there,
To oppose his hatred fully.   Welcome home.   20

            Enter Sicinius and Brutus.

Behold! these are the tribunes of the people,
The tongues o' the common mouth: I do despise them;
For they do prank them in authority
Against all noble sufferance.

    Sic.   Pass no further.   24

    Cor. Ha! what is that?

    Bru. It will be dangerous to go on: no further.

    Cor. What makes this change?

    Men.   The matter?   27

    Com. Hath he not pass'd the noble and the common?

    Bru. Cominius, no.

    Cor.   Have I had children's voices?

16 To . . . restitution: *beyond hope of redemption*
23 prank them: *deck themselves*

Senat. Tribunes, give way; he shall to the market-
place.

Bru. The people are incens'd against him.

Sic. Stop,
Or all will fall in broil.

Cor. Are these your herd? 32
Must these have voices, that can yield them now,
And straight disclaim their tongues? What are your
offices?
You being their mouths, why rule you not their teeth?
Have you not set them on?

Men. Be calm, be calm. 36

Cor. It is a purpos'd thing, and grows by plot,
To curb the will of the nobility:
Suffer 't, and live with such as cannot rule
Nor ever will be rul'd.

Bru. Call 't not a plot: 40
The people cry you mock'd them, and of late,
When corn was given them gratis, you repin'd;
Scandal'd the suppliants for the people, call'd them
Time-pleasers, flatterers, foes to nobleness. 44

Cor. Why, this was known before.

Bru. Not to them all.

Cor. Have you inform'd them sithence?

Bru. How! I inform them!

Cor. You are like to do such business.

Bru. Not unlike,
Each way, to better yours. 48

Cor. Why then should I be consul? By yond clouds,
Let me deserve so ill as you, and make me
Your fellow tribune.

37 purpos'd: *premeditated*   43 Scandal'd: *slandered*
46 sithence: *since*
48 Each . . . yours: *to surpass your doings in every way*

Sic.   You show too much of that
For which the people stir; if you will pass   52
To where you are bound, you must inquire your way,
Which you are out of, with a gentler spirit;
Or never be so noble as a consul,
Nor yoke with him for tribune.
    Men.   Let's be calm.   56
    Com. The people are abus'd; set on. This palt'ring
Becomes not Rome, nor has Coriolanus
Deserv'd this so dishonour'd rub, laid falsely
I' the plain way of his merit.
    Cor.   Tell me of corn! 60
This was my speech, and I will speak 't again,—
    Men. Not now, not now.
    Senat.   Not in this heat, sir, now.
    Cor. Now, as I live, I will. My nobler friends,
I crave their pardons: 64
For the mutable, rank-scented meiny, let them
Regard me as I do not flatter, and
Therein behold themselves: I say again,
In soothing them we nourish 'gainst our senate   68
The cockle of rebellion, insolence, sedition,
Which we ourselves have plough'd for, sow'd and scatter'd,
By mingling them with us, the honour'd number;
Who lack not virtue, no, nor power, but that   72
Which they have given to beggars.
    Men.   Well, no more.
    Senat. No more words, we beseech you.

---

51 that: *that defect of character*   56 yoke: *join in service*
57 abus'd: *deceived*   set on: *incited*
59 dishonour'd rub: *shameful obstruction*   falsely: *treacherously*
65 meiny: *multitude*
66 Regard . . . flatter: *heed my unflattering presentation*
69 cockle: *noxious weed*

   Cor.   How! no more!
As for my country I have shed my blood,
Not fearing outward force, so shall my lungs   76
Coin words till their decay against those measles,
Which we disdain should tetter us, yet sought
The very way to catch them.
   Bru.   You speak o' the people,
As if you were a god to punish, not   80
A man of their infirmity.
   Sic.   'Twere well
We let the people know 't.
   Men.   What, what? his choler?
   Cor. Choler!
Were I as patient as the midnight sleep,   84
By Jove, 'twould be my mind!
   Sic.   It is a mind
That shall remain a poison where it is,
Not poison any further.
   Cor.   Shall remain!
Hear you this Triton of the minnows? mark you   88
His absolute 'Shall'?
   Com.   'Twas from the canon.
   Cor.   'Shall!'
O good but most unwise patricians! why,
You grave but reckless senators, have you thus
Given Hydra here to choose an officer,   92
That with his peremptory 'shall,' being but
The horn and noise o' the monster's, wants not spirit
To say he'll turn your current in a ditch,
And make your channel his? If he have power,   96

77 measles: *disease spots*   78 tetter: *form an eruption on*
85 mind: *resolved opinion*   88 Triton: *sea-god*
89 from the canon: *not authorized by law*
92 Given: *allowed*   Hydra: *the many-headed monster*
94 horn and noise: *noisy horn*

Then vail your ignorance; if none, awake
Your dangerous lenity.   If you are learn'd,
Be not as common fools; if you are not,
Let them have cushions by you.   You are plebeians 100
If they be senators; and they are no less,
When, both your voices blended, the great'st taste
Most palates theirs.   They choose their magistrate,
And such a one as he, who puts his 'shall,'   104
His popular 'shall,' against a graver bench
Than ever frown'd in Greece.   By Jove himself!
It makes the consuls base; and my soul aches
To know, when two authorities are up,   108
Neither supreme, how soon confusion
May enter 'twixt the gap of both and take
The one by th' other.

   Com.   Well, on to the market-place.

   Cor. Whoever gave that counsel, to give forth   112
The corn o' the store-house gratis, as 'twas us'd
Sometime in Greece,—

   Men.   Well, well; no more of that.

   Cor. Though there the people had more absolute
      power,
I say, they nourish'd disobedience, fed   116
The ruin of the state.

   Bru.   Why, shall the people give
One that speaks thus their voice?

   Cor.   I'll give my reasons,
More worthier than their voices.   They know the corn
Was not our recompense, resting well assur'd   120
They ne'er did service for 't.   Being press'd to the war,

97 vail . . . ignorance: *let your folly submit*
97, 98 awake . . . lenity: *arouse yourselves from your dangerous
    mildness*   100 cushions: *i.e. seats in the Senate*
102 great'st taste: *predominant taste*   103 palates: *smacks of*
108 up: *established*   110 gap of both: *cleavage between the two*
110, 111 take . . . other: *use the one to overthrow the other*
120 our recompense: *fair payment from us*   121 press'd: *enlisted*

Even when the navel of the state was touch'd,
They would not thread the gates: this kind of service
Did not deserve corn gratis. Being i' the war,   124
Their mutinies and revolts, wherein they show'd
Most valour, spoke not for them.   Th' accusation
Which they have often made against the senate,
All cause unborn, could never be the motive   128
Of our so frank donation. Well, what then?
How shall this bosom multiplied digest
The senate's courtesy?   Let deeds express
What's like to be their words: 'We did request it;   132
We are the greater poll, and in true fear
They gave us our demands.'   Thus we debase
The nature of our seats, and make the rabble
Call our cares fears; which will in time break ope   136
The locks o' the senate, and bring in the crows
To peck the eagles.
    Men.   Come, enough.
    Bru. Enough, with over-measure.
    Cor.   No, take more:
What may be sworn by, both divine and human,   140
Seal what I end withal! This double worship,
Where one part does disdain with cause, the other
Insult without all reason; where gentry, title, wisdom,
Cannot conclude, but by the yea and no   144
Of general ignorance,—it must omit
Real necessities, and give way the while
To unstable slightness: purpose so barr'd, it follows

122 navel: *vital center*   123 thread: *pass through*
128 All . . . unborn: *causelessly*   motive: *occasion; cf. n.*
130 bosom multiplied; *cf. n.*
131, 132 Let . . . words: *let their actions explain what they are likely
    to say*   133 poll: *number*
139 over-measure: *excess*
140, 141 What . . . withal: *may all divine and human sanctities attest
    my final assertion*   144 conclude: *come to a decision*
147 unstable slightness: *petty whims*   purpose so barr'd: *where
    rational action is thus obstructed*

Nothing is done to purpose.   Therefore, beseech
   you,—   148
You that will be less fearful than discreet,
That love the fundamental part of state
More than you doubt the change on 't, that prefer
A noble life before a long, and wish   152
To jump a body with a dangerous physic
That's sure of death without it, at once pluck out
The multitudinous tongue; let them not lick
The sweet which is their poison.   Your dishonour   156
Mangles true judgment, and bereaves the state
Of that integrity which should become 't,
Not having the power to do the good it would,
For th' ill which doth control 't.
   Bru.   H'as said enough. 160
   Sic. H'as spoken like a traitor, and shall answer
As traitors do.
   Cor. Thou wretch! despite o'erwhelm thee!   163
What should the people do with these bald tribunes?
On whom depending, their obedience fails
To the greater bench.   In a rebellion,
When what's not meet, but what must be, was law,
Then were they chosen: in a better hour,   168
Let what is meet be said it must be meet,
And throw their power i' the dust.
   Bru. Manifest treason!
   Sic.   This a consul? no.
   Bru. The ædiles, ho!

149 less . . . discreet: *prudent rather than timid*
150, 151 That . . . on 't: *whose devotion to the essentials of good
government exceeds your fear of innovations in politics*
153 jump: *put in hazard*
155 multitudinous tongue: *i.e. voting power of the rabble*
160 H'as: *he has*   161 answer: *abide the penalty*
163 despite: *malice*   166 greater bench: *senate*
167 what's . . . be: *inevitable necessity, however unfitting*
172 ædiles: *ædiles of the people, assistants to the tribunes*

Enter an Ædile.

               Let him be apprehended. 172

Sic. Go, call the people; [*Exit Ædile.*] in whose
   name, myself
Attach thee as a traitorous innovator,
A foe to the public weal: obey, I charge thee,
And follow to thine answer.

    Cor.   Hence, old goat!   176

    All. We'll surety him.

    Com.   Ag'd sir, hands off.

    Cor. Hence, rotten thing! or I shall shake thy bones
Out of thy garments.

    Sic.   Help, ye citizens!

Enter a rabble of Plebeians with the Ædiles.

    Men. On both sides more respect.   180

    Sic. Here's he that would take from you all your
   power.

    Bru. Seize him, ædiles!

    All. Down with him!—down with him!—

    2. Sen. Weapons!—weapons!—weapons!—   184

               They all bustle about Coriolanus.

Tribunes!—patricians!—citizens!—What ho!—
Sicinius!—Brutus!—Coriolanus!—Citizens!

    All. Peace!—Peace!—Peace!—Stay!—Hold!—
   Peace!

    Men. What is about to be?—I am out of breath; 188
Confusion's near; I cannot speak. You, tribunes
To the people! Coriolanus, patience!
Speak, good Sicinius.

    Sic.   Hear me, people; peace!

    All. Let's hear our tribune:—Peace!— Speak,
   speak, speak.   192

174 Attach: *arrest*   innovator: *agitator*   177 surety: *vouch for*

Sic. You are at point to lose your liberties:
Martius would have all from you; Martius,
Whom late you have nam'd for consul.

Men.   Fie, fie, fie!
This is the way to kindle, not to quench.   196

   Sen. To unbuild the city and to lay all flat.

   Sic. What is the city but the people?

   All.   True,
The people are the city.

   Bru. By the consent of all, we were establish'd   200
The people's magistrates.

   All.   You so remain.

   Men. And so are like to do.

   Com. That is the way to lay the city flat;
To bring the roof to the foundation,   204
And bury all, which yet distinctly ranges,
In heaps and piles of ruin.

   Sic.   This deserves death.

   Bru. Or let us stand to our authority,
Or let us lose it.   We do here pronounce,   208
Upon the part o' the people, in whose power
We were elected theirs, Martius is worthy
Of present death.

   Sic.   Therefore lay hold of him;
Bear him to the rock Tarpeian, and from thence   212
Into destruction cast him.

   Bru.   Ædiles, seize him!

   All Ple. Yield, Martius, yield!

   Men.   Hear me one word;
Beseech you, tribunes, hear me but a word.

   Æd. Peace, peace!   216

   Men. Be that you seem, truly your country's friends,

---

205 distinctly ranges: *stretches out intact in separate buildings*
212 rock Tarpeian; *cf. n.*

And temperately proceed to what you would
Thus violently redress.

Bru.   Sir, those cold ways,
That seem like prudent helps, are very poisonous   220
Where the disease is violent.   Lay hands upon him,
And bear him to the rock.

Coriolanus draws his sword.

Cor.   No, I'll die here.
There's some among you have beheld me fighting:
Come, try upon yourselves what you have seen me.   224

Men. Down with that sword!   Tribunes, withdraw
        awhile.

Bru. Lay hands upon him.

Men.   Help Martius, help,
You that be noble; help him, young and old!

All. Down with him!—down with him!   228

Exeunt.

*In this mutiny the Tribunes, the Ædiles, and
        the People are beat in.*

Men. Go, get you to your house; begone, away!
All will be naught else.

2. Sen.   Get you gone.

Cor.   Stand fast;
We have as many friends as enemies.

Men. Shall it be put to that?

Sen.   The gods forbid!   232
I prithee, noble friend, home to thy house;
Leave us to cure this cause.

Men.   For 'tis a sore upon us
You cannot tent yourself: begone, beseech you.

Com. Come, sir, along with us.   236

Cor. I would they were barbarians,—as they are,

224 seen me: *seen me do*   230 naught: *ruined*
234 cause: *disorder, disease*

Though in Rome litter'd,—not Romans,—as they are
    not,
Though calv'd i' the porch o' the Capitol,—
  Men.   Begone;
Put not your worthy rage into your tongue;   240
One time will owe another.
  Cor.   On fair ground
I could beat forty of them.
  Men.   I could myself
Take up a brace o' the best of them; yea, the two
    tribunes.
  Com. But now 'tis odds beyond arithmetic;   244
And manhood is call'd foolery when it stands
Against a falling fabric. Will you hence,
Before the tag return? whose rage doth rend
Like interrupted waters and o'erbear   248
What they are us'd to bear.
  Men.   Pray you, begone.
I'll try whether my old wit be in request
With those that have but little: this must be patch'd
With cloth of any colour.
  Com.   Nay, come away.   252
           Exeunt Coriolanus and Cominius.
  Patri. This man has marr'd his fortune.
  Men. His nature is too noble for the world:
He would not flatter Neptune for his trident,
Or Jove for 's power to thunder. His heart's his
    mouth: 256
What his breast forges, that his tongue must vent;

238 litter'd: *whelped, born like beasts*
241 One . . . another: *a balance will be struck between this unlucky
    time and one that will be more favorable*
244 beyond arithmetic: *incalculable*   246 fabric: *building*
247 tag: *rabble*   248 interrupted: *obstructed*
251, 252 this . . . colour: *we must use the roughest remedies*

And, being angry, does forget that ever
He heard the name of death.   *A noise within.*
Here's goodly work!

   Patri.   I would they were a-bed! 260

   Men. I would they were in Tiber! What the ven-
      geance!
Could he not speak 'em fair?

   Enter Brutus and Sicinius with the rabble again.

   Sic.   Where is this viper
That would depopulate the city and
Be every man himself?

   Men.   You worthy tribunes,— 264

   Sic. He shall be thrown down the Tarpeian rock
With rigorous hands: he hath resisted law,
And therefore law shall scorn him further trial
Than the severity of the public power,   268
Which he so sets at nought.

   1. Cit.   He shall well know
The noble tribunes are the people's mouths,
And we their hands.

   All.   He shall, sure on 't.

   Men.   Sir, sir,—

   Sic. Peace!   272

   Men. Do not cry havoc, where you should but hunt
With modest warrant.

   Sic.   Sir, how comes 't that you
Have holp to make this rescue?

   Men.   Hear me speak:
As I do know the consul's worthiness,   276
So can I name his faults.

   Sic.   Consul! what consul?

258 does: *he does*   262 speak 'em fair: *conciliate them*
268 severity: *i.e. exposure to severity*
273 cry havoc: *give the signal for indiscriminate slaughter*
274 With . . . warrant: *as moderation warrants*

Men. The Consul Coriolanus.

Bru.   He consul!

All. No, no, no, no, no.

Men. If, by the tribunes' leave, and yours, good
    people,   280
I may be heard, I would crave a word or two,
The which shall turn you to no further harm
Than so much loss of time.

Sic.   Speak briefly then;
For we are peremptory to dispatch   284
This viperous traitor. To eject him, hence
Were but one danger, and to keep him here
Our certain death; therefore it is decreed
He dies to-night.

Men.   Now the good gods forbid   288
That our renowned Rome, whose gratitude
Towards her deserved children is enroll'd
In Jove's own book, like an unnatural dam
Should now eat up her own!   292

Sic. He's a disease that must be cut away.

Men. O! he's a limb that has but a disease;
Mortal to cut it off; to cure it easy.
What has he done to Rome that's worthy death?   296
Killing our enemies, the blood he hath lost,—
Which, I dare vouch, is more than that he hath
By many an ounce,—he dropp'd it for his country;
And what is left, to lose it by his country,   300
Were to us all, that do 't and suffer it,
A brand to th' end o' the world.

Sic.   This is clean kam.

Bru. Merely awry: when he did love his country

282 turn you to: *occasion you*
291 dam: *mother (of beasts)*
301 suffer: *permit*
302 brand: *mark of infamy*
303 Merely: *completely*

284 peremptory: *resolved*
295 Mortal: *producing death*

clean kam: *absolutely perverse*

It honour'd him.

    Men.   The service of the foot,   304
Being once gangren'd, is not then respected
For what before it was.

    Bru.   We'll hear no more.
Pursue him to his house, and pluck him thence,
Lest his infection, being of catching nature,   308
Spread further.

    Men.   One word more, one word.
This tiger-footed rage, when it shall find
The harm of unscann'd swiftness, will, too late,
Tie leaden pounds to 's heels.   Proceed by process; 312
Lest parties—as he is belov'd—break out,
And sack great Rome with Romans.

    Bru.   If it were so,—

    Sic. What do ye talk?
Have we not had a taste of his obedience?   316
Our ædiles smote? ourselves resisted?   Come!

    Men. Consider this: he has been bred i' the wars
Since a' could draw a sword, and is ill school'd
In bolted language; meal and bran together   320
He throws without distinction.   Give me leave,
I'll go to him, and undertake to bring him
Where he shall answer by a lawful form,—
In peace,—to his utmost peril.

    1. Sen.   Noble tribunes,   324
It is the humane way: the other course
Will prove too bloody, and the end of it
Unknown to the beginning.

    Sic.   Noble Menenius,
Be you then as the people's officer.   328
Masters, lay down your weapons.

304-306 The . . . was; *cf. n.*   311 unscann'd: *rash, thoughtless*
312 pounds: *pound-weights*   process: *legal method*
313 parties: *factions*   315 talk: *say*   320 bolted: *sifted*

   Bru.   Go not home.
   Sic. Meet on the market-place.   We'll attend you
      there:
Where, if you bring not Martius, we'll proceed
In our first way.   332
   Men. I'll bring him to you.
[*To the Senators.*] Let me desire your company.   He
      must come,
Or what is worst will follow.
   Sen.   Pray you, let's to him.
                            Exeunt omnes.

Scene Two

[*The Same.   A Room in Coriolanus's House*]

Enter Coriolanus with Nobles.

   Cor. Let them pull all about mine ears; present me
Death on the wheel, or at wild horses' heels;
Or pile ten hills on the Tarpeian rock,
That the precipitation might down stretch   4
Below the beam of sight; yet will I still
Be thus to them.
   Noble.   You do the nobler.
   Cor. I muse my mother
Does not approve me further, who was wont   8
To call them woollen vassals, things created
To buy and sell with groats, to show bare heads
In congregations, to yawn, be still, and wonder,
When one but of my ordinance stood up   12
To speak of peace or war.

---

4 precipitation: *steepness*
5 Below . . . sight: *lower than eyesight can reach*
7 muse: *wonder*   9 woollen vassals: *coarsely dressed underlings*
10 groats: *four-penny coins*   12 ordinance: *rank*

Enter Volumnia.

           I talk of you:
Why did you wish me milder? Would you have me
False to my nature? Rather say I play
The man I am.
    Vol.   O! sir, sir, sir,   16
I would have had you put your power well on
Before you had worn it out.
    Cor.   Let go.
    Vol. You might have been enough the man you are
With striving less to be so: lesser had been   20
The thwartings of your dispositions if
You had not show'd them how you were dispos'd,
Ere they lack'd power to cross you.
    Cor.   Let them hang.
    Vol. Ay, and burn too.   24

Enter Menenius with the Senators.

    Men. Come, come; you have been too rough, some-
        thing too rough;
You must return and mend it.
    Sen.   There's no remedy;
Unless, by not so doing, our good city
Cleave in the midst, and perish.
    Vol.   Pray be counsell'd. 28
I have a heart as little apt as yours,
But yet a brain that leads my use of anger
To better vantage.
    Men.   Well said, noble woman!
Before he should thus stoop to the herd, but that   32
The violent fit o' the time craves it as physic
For the whole state, I would put mine armour on,

18 Let go: *No more of that*   21 thwartings; *cf. n.*
28 Cleave . . . midst: *break in two*
29 as little apt: *as unbending*   32 but: *except*

Which I can scarcely bear.

Cor.   What must I do?

Men. Return to the tribunes.

Cor.   Well, what then? what then? 36

Men. Repent what you have spoke.

Cor. For them! I cannot do it to the gods;
Must I then do 't to them?

Vol.   You are too absolute;
Though therein you can never be too noble,   40
But when extremities speak. I have heard you say,
Honour and policy, like unsever'd friends,
I' the war do grow together: grant that, and tell me,
In peace what each of them by th' other lose,   44
That they combine not there.

Cor.   Tush, tush!

Men.   A good demand.

Vol. If it be honour in your wars to seem
The same you are not,—which, for your best ends,
You adopt your policy,—how is it less or worse,   48
That it shall hold companionship in peace
With honour, as in war, since that to both
It stands in like request?

Cor.   Why force you this?

Vol. Because that now it lies you on to speak   52
To the people; not by your own instruction,
Nor by the matter which your heart prompts you,
But with such words that are but rooted in
Your tongue, though but bastards and syllables   56
Of no allowance to your bosom's truth.

39 absolute: *positive, peremptory*
41 But . . . speak: *except under the command of necessity*
42 policy: *craft*   45 combine: *join*   48 adopt: *adopt as*
51 stands . . . request: *is equally valuable*   force: *urge*
52 lies . . . on: *is incumbent upon you*
53 by . . . instruction: *as your nature teaches you*
55, 56 are . . . tongue: *have their roots no deeper than your tongue;*
  cf. n.   57 of . . . to: *unapproved by*

Now this no more dishonours you at all
Than to take in a town with gentle words,
Which else would put you to your fortune and   60
The hazard of much blood.
I would dissemble with my nature where
My fortunes and my friends at stake requir'd
I should do so in honour: I am in this,   64
Your wife, your son, these senators, the nobles;
And you will rather show our general louts
How you can frown than spend a fawn upon 'em,
For the inheritance of their loves and safeguard   68
Of what that want might ruin.
    Men.   Noble lady!
Come, go with us; speak fair; you may salve so,
Not what is dangerous present, but the loss
Of what is past.
    Vol.   I prithee now, my son,   72
Go to them, with this bonnet in thy hand;
And thus far having stretch'd it,—here be with them,—
Thy knee bussing the stones,—for in such business
Action is eloquence, and the eyes of th' ignorant   76
More learned than the ears,—waving thy head,
Which often, thus, correcting thy stout heart,
Now humble as the ripest mulberry
That will not hold the handling: or say to them,   80
Thou art their soldier, and being bred in broils
Hast not the soft way which, thou dost confess,
Were fit for thee to use as they to claim,

59 take in. *get possession of*
60 put . . . fortune: *force you to risk the fortune of war*
64 I am: *I am at stake*
66 general louts: *the good-for-nothings of the community*
68 safeguard: *for the security*
69 that want: *the want of their loves*   71, 72 Not . . . past; *cf. n.*
73 this bonnet: *that which Coriolanus wears*
74, 75 And . . . stones; *cf. n.*
78 Which often: *a conciliatory gesture which you are to repeat often*
83 as they: *as for them*

In asking their good loves; but thou wilt frame   84
Thyself, forsooth, hereafter theirs, so far
As thou hast power and person.

Men.   This but done,
Even as she speaks, why, their hearts were yours;
For they have pardons, being ask'd, as free   88
As words to little purpose.

Vol.   Prithee now,
Go, and be rul'd; although I know thou hadst rather
Follow thine enemy in a fiery gulf
Than flatter him in a bower.

Enter Cominius.

                        Here is Cominius.   92
Com. I have been i' the market-place; and, sir, 'tis fit
You make strong party, or defend yourself
By calmness or by absence: all's in anger.

Men. Only fair speech.

Com.   I think 'twill serve, if he 96
Can thereto frame his spirit.

Vol.   He must, and will.
Prithee now, say you will, and go about it.

Cor. Must I go show them my unbarbed sconce?
Must I with my base tongue give to my noble heart 100
A lie that it must bear? Well, I will do 't:
Yet, were there but this single plot to lose,
This mould of Martius, they to dust should grind it,
And throw 't against the wind.   To the market-
        place!   104
You have put me now to such a part which never
I shall discharge to the life.

87 were: *would be*   88 free: *abundantly*
92 bower: *abode of pleasure*
94 make . . . party: *collect many supporters*
99 unbarbed sconce: *bared head*
102 this single plot: *my own person*
105 which: *as*   106 discharge . . . life: *perform naturally*

 Com.   Come, come, we'll prompt you.
 Vol. I prithee now, sweet son, as thou hast said
My praises made thee first a soldier, so,   108
To have my praise for this, perform a part
Thou hast not done before.
 Cor.   Well, I must do 't:
Away, my disposition, and possess me
Some harlot's spirit! My throat of war be turn'd, 112
Which quir'd with my drum, into a pipe
Small as an eunuch, or the virgin voice
That babies lulls asleep! The smiles of knaves
Tent in my cheeks, and school-boys' tears take up 116
The glasses of my sight! A beggar's tongue
Make motion through my lips, and my arm'd knees,
Who bow'd but in my stirrup, bend like his
That hath receiv'd an alms! I will not do 't, 120
Lest I surcease to honour mine own truth,
And by my body's action teach my mind
A most inherent baseness.
 Vol.   At thy choice then:
To beg of thee it is my more dishonour   124
Than thou of them. Come all to ruin; let
Thy mother rather feel thy pride than fear
Thy dangerous stoutness, for I mock at death
With as big heart as thou. Do as thou list, 128
Thy valiantness was mine, thou suck'dst it from me,
But owe thy pride thyself.
 Cor.   Pray, be content:
Mother, I am going to the market-place;

113 quir'd: *harmonized*   114 virgin: *nurse-maid's*
116 Tent: *encamp* take up: *fill* 117 The . . . sight: *my eyes*
121 surcease to honour: *cease to have respect for*
124 my . . . dishonour: *more dishonor for me*
125 thou: *for thee to beg*
125-127 let . . . stoutness: *let my anxiety concerning thy dangerous*
  obstinacy give place to such pride as thou feelest
130 owe: *own*

Chide me no more. I'll mountebank their loves,   132
Cog their hearts from them, and come home belov'd
Of all the trades in Rome. Look, I am going:
Commend me to my wife. I'll return consul,
Or never trust to what my tongue can do   136
I' the way of flattery further.

   Vol.   Do your will.

                           Exit Volumnia.

   Com. Away! the tribunes do attend you: arm your-
     self
To answer mildly; for they are prepar'd
With accusations, as I hear, more strong   140
Than are upon you yet.

   Cor. The word is 'mildly.' Pray you, let us go:
Let them accuse me by invention, I
Will answer in mine honour.

   Men.   Ay, but mildly.   144

   Cor. Well, mildly be it then. Mildly!   *Exeunt.*

Scene Three

[*The Same.   The Forum*]

Enter Sicinius and Brutus.

   Bru. In this point charge him home, that he affects
Tyrannical power: if he evade us there,
Enforce him with his envy to the people,
And that the spoil got on the Antiates   4
Was ne'er distributed.—

            Enter an Ædile.

What, will he come?

132 mountebank: *act the quack-vendor for*   133 Cog: *cheat*
138 arm yourself: *prepare*   1 affects: *aims at*
3 Enforce: *press*   4 on: *at the expense of*

Æd.   He's coming.

Bru.   How accompanied?

Æd. With old Menenius, and those senators
That always favour'd him.

Sic.   Have you a catalogue   8
Of all the voices that we have procur'd,
Set down by the poll?

Æd.   I have; 'tis ready.

Sic. Have you collected them by tribes?

Æd.   I have.

Sic. Assemble presently the people hither;   12
And when they hear me say, 'It shall be so,
I' the right and strength o' the commons,' be it either
For death, for fine, or banishment, then let them,
If I say, fine, cry 'fine,'—if death, cry 'death,'   16
Insisting on the old prerogative
And power i' the truth o' the cause.

Æd.   I shall inform them.

Bru. And when such time they have begun to cry,
Let them not cease, but with a din confus'd   20
Enforce the present execution
Of what we chance to sentence.

Æd.   Very well.

Sic. Make them be strong and ready for this hint,
When we shall hap to give 't them.

Bru.   Go about it.   24

[*Exit Ædile.*]

Put him to choler straight.   He hath been us'd
Ever to conquer, and to have his worth
Of contradiction: being once chaf'd, he cannot
Be rein'd again to temperance; then he speaks   28

10 by the poll: *by individual names*
11 by tribes; *cf. n.*   21 present: *immediate*
26, 27 have . . . contradiction: *indulge his love of contradiction in full
measure*

What's in his heart; and that is there which looks
With us to break his neck.

*Enter Coriolanus, Menenius, and Cominius, with
others.*

Sic.   Well, here he comes.
Men. Calmly, I do beseech you.
Cor. Ay, as an hostler, that for the poorest piece   32
Will bear the knave by the volume.   The honour'd gods
Keep Rome in safety, and the chairs of justice
Supplied with worthy men! plant love among 's!
Throng our large temples with the shows of peace,   36
And not our streets with war!
1. Sen.   Amen, amen.
Men. A noble wish.

Enter the Ædile with the Plebeians.

Sic.   Draw near, ye people.
Æd. List to your tribunes; audience; peace! I say.
Cor. First, hear me speak.
Both Tri.   Well, say.   Peace, ho! 40
Cor. Shall I be charg'd no further than this present?
Must all determine here?
Sic.   I do demand,
If you submit you to the people's voices,
Allow their officers, and are content   44
To suffer lawful censure for such faults
As shall be prov'd upon you?
Cor.   I am content.
Men. Lo! citizens, he says he is content:
The warlike service he has done, consider; think   48
Upon the wounds his body bears, which show

29 looks: *tends, is calculated*   32 piece: *coin*
33 bear . . . volume: *submit to be called knave interminably*
41 this present: *the present occasion*
42 determine: *end*   44 Allow: *acknowledge*

Like graves i' the holy churchyard.

    Cor.   Scratches with briers,
Scars to move laughter only.

    Men.   Consider further,
That when he speaks not like a citizen,   52
You find him like a soldier: do not take
His rougher accents for malicious sounds,
But, as I say, such as become a soldier,
Rather than envy you.

    Com.   Well, well; no more.   56

    Cor. What is the matter,
That being pass'd for consul with full voice
I am so dishonour'd that the very hour
You take it off again?

    Sic.   Answer to us.   60

    Cor. Say, then: 'tis true, I ought so.

    Sic. We charge you, that you have contriv'd to take
From Rome all season'd office, and to wind
Yourself into a power tyrannical;   64
For which you are a traitor to the people.

    Cor. How! Traitor!

    Men.   Nay, temperately; your promise.

    Cor. The fires i' the lowest hell fold in the people!
Call me their traitor! Thou injurious tribune!   68
Within thine eyes sat twenty thousand deaths,
In thy hands clutch'd as many millions, in
Thy lying tongue both numbers, I would say
'Thou liest' unto thee with a voice as free   72
As I do pray the gods.

    Sic.   Mark you this, people?

    All. To the rock!—to the rock with him!

54 accents; *cf. n.*
62 contriv'd: *designed*
67 fold in: *encompass*
69 Within: *although within*

56 envy: *evidence hostility to*
63 season'd: *time-honored*
68 injurious: *insulting*

Sic.　　　　　　　　　　　　　Peace!
We need not put new matter to his charge:
What you have seen him do, and heard him speak,　76
Beating your officers, cursing yourselves,
Opposing laws with strokes, and here defying
Those whose great power must try him; even this,
So criminal and in such capital kind,　　　80
Deserves th' extremest death.
　　Bru.　　　　　　　　But since he hath
Serv'd well for Rome,—
　　Cor.　　　　　　What do you prate of service?
　　Bru. I talk of that, that know it.
　　Cor.　　　　　　　　You!
　　Men. Is this the promise that you made your
　　　mother?　　　　　　　　　84
　　Com. Know, I pray you,—
　　Cor.　　　　　　　I'll know no further:
Let them pronounce the steep Tarpeian death,
Vagabond exile, flaying, pent to linger
But with a grain a day, I would not buy　　88
Their mercy at the price of one fair word,
Nor check my courage for what they can give,
To have 't with saying 'Good morrow.'
　　Sic.　　　　　　　For that he has,—
As much as in him lies,—from time to time　92
Envied against the people, seeking means
To pluck away their power, as now at last
Given hostile strokes, and that not in the presence
Of dreaded justice, but on the ministers　　96
That doth distribute it; in the name o' the people,
And in the power of us the tribunes, we,

80 capital kind: *death-deserving measure*
87 pent: *imprisoned*　　　linger: *starve slowly*
91 To have 't: *though I could have it*
93 Envied: *been malignant*　　　　　95 not: *not merely*
97 doth: *do; cf. n.*

Even from this instant, banish him our city,
In peril of precipitation   100
From off the rock Tarpeian, never more
To enter our Rome gates: i' the people's name,
I say, it shall be so.
    All. It shall be so.—It shall be so.—Let him
      away.—   104
He's banish'd, and it shall be so.
    Com. Hear me, my masters, and my common
      friends,—
    Sic. He's sentenc'd; no more hearing.
    Com.   Let me speak:
I have been consul, and can show for Rome   108
Her enemies' marks upon me.   I do love
My country's good with a respect more tender,
More holy, and profound, than mine own life,
My dear wife's estimate, her womb's increase,   112
And treasure of my loins; then if I would
Speak that—
    Sic.   We know your drift: speak what?
    Bru. There's no more to be said but he is banish'd,
As enemy to the people and his country.   116
It shall be so.
    All.   It shall be so,—it shall be so.
    Cor. You common cry of curs! whose breath I hate
As reek o' the rotten fens, whose loves I prize
As the dead carcasses of unburied men   120
That do corrupt my air, I banish you;
And here remain with your uncertainty!
Let every feeble rumour shake your hearts!
Your enemies, with nodding of their plumes,   124
Fan you into despair!   Have the power still

112 estimate: *reputation*
122 remain: *do you remain*   uncertainty: *inconstancy of mind*

To banish your defenders; till at length
Your ignorance,—which finds not till it feels,—
Making but reservation of yourselves,—   128
Still your own foes,—deliver you as most
Abated captives to some nation
That won you without blows! Despising,
For you, the city, thus I turn my back: 132
There is a world elsewhere.

> *Exeunt Coriolanus, Cominius with others.*
> *They all shout and throw up their caps.*

  Æd. The people's enemy is gone, is gone!
  All. Our enemy is banish'd!—he is gone!—Hoo! oo!
  Sic. Go, see him out at gates, and follow him,   136
As he hath follow'd you, with all despite;
Give him deserv'd vexation. Let a guard
Attend us through the city.   139
  All. Come, come,—let's see him out at gates! come!
The gods preserve our noble tribunes! Come!

> *Exeunt.*

ACT FOURTH

Scene One

[*Rome.   Before a Gate of the City*]

*Enter Coriolanus, Volumnia, Virgilia, Menenius, Co-
    minius, with the young Nobility of Rome.*

  Cor. Come, leave your tears: a brief farewell: the
    beast
With many heads butts me away.   Nay, mother,
Where is your ancient courage? you were us'd

128 Making . . . of: *exempting from banishment none but*
130 Abated: *crestfallen*   133 S. d. with others; *cf. n.*

To say extremity was the trier of spirits;   4
That common chances common men could bear;
That when the sea was calm all boats alike
Show'd mastership in floating; fortune's blows,
When most struck home,—being gentle, wounded,
    craves   8
A noble cunning: you were us'd to load me
With precepts that would make invincible
The heart that conn'd them.
   Vir. O heavens! O heavens!
   Cor.   Nay, I prithee, woman,— 12
   Vol. Now the red pestilence strike all trades in
    Rome,
And occupations perish!
   Cor.   What, what, what!
I shall be lov'd when I am lack'd. Nay, mother,
Resume that spirit, when you were wont to say,   16
If you had been the wife of Hercules,
Six of his labours you'd have done, and sav'd
Your husband so much sweat. Cominius,
Droop not; adieu. Farewell, my wife! my mother! 20
I'll do well yet. Thou old and true Menenius,
Thy tears are salter than a younger man's,
And venomous to thine eyes. My sometime general,
I have seen thee stern, and thou hast oft beheld   24
Heart-hardening spectacles; tell these sad women
'Tis fond to wail inevitable strokes
As 'tis to laugh at 'em. My mother, you wot well
My hazards still have been your solace; and   28
Believe 't not lightly,—though I go alone
Like to a lonely dragon, that his fen
Makes fear'd and talk'd of more than seen,—your son

7-9 fortune's . . . cunning; *cf. n.*   13 red pestilence: *plague*
14 occupations: *mechanical employments*   16 Resume: *recover*
26 fond: *as fond, as foolish*

Will or exceed the common or be caught   32
With cautelous baits and practice.
  Vol.   My first son,
Whither wilt thou go?   Take good Cominius
With thee awhile: determine on some course,
More than a wild exposture to each chance   36
That starts i' the way before thee.
  Cor.   O the gods !
  Com. I'll follow thee a month, devise with thee
Where thou shalt rest, that thou mayst hear of us,
And we of thee: so, if the time thrust forth   40
A cause for thy repeal, we shall not send
O'er the vast world to seek a single man,
And lose advantage, which doth ever cool
I' the absence of the needer.
  Cor.   Fare ye well: 44
Thou hast years upon thee; and thou art too full
Of the wars' surfeits, to go rove with one
That's yet unbruis'd: bring me but out at gate.
Come, my sweet wife, my dearest mother, and   48
My friends of noble touch, when I am forth,
Bid me farewell, and smile.   I pray you, come.
While I remain above the ground you shall
Hear from me still; and never of me aught   52
But what is like me formerly.
  Men.   That's worthily
As any ear can hear.   Come, let's not weep.
If I could shake off but one seven years

---

32 or . . . common: *either do some deed of fame*
33 With . . . practice: *by the snares and treachery of wily adversaries*
   first: *first and only, eminent*   36 exposture: *exposure*
41 repeal: *recall*
43 advantage: *opportunity to profit by circumstances*
44 needer: *him who should utilize the advantage*
46 wars' surfeits: *strains from military service*
49 noble touch: *proved nobility*
53 me formerly: *my former self*   worthily: *as worthily spoken*

From these old arms and legs, by the good gods,   56
I'd with thee every foot.
    Cor.   Give me thy hand:
Come.   *Exeunt.*

Scene Two

[*The Same.   A Street near the Gate*]

Enter the two Tribunes, Sicinius and Brutus, with the
Ædile.

    Sic. Bid them all home; he's gone, and we'll no
    further.
The nobility are vex'd, whom we see have sided
In his behalf.
    Bru.   Now we have shown our power,
Let us seem humbler after it is done   4
Than when it was a-doing.
    Sic.   Bid them home;
Say their great enemy is gone, and they
Stand in their ancient strength.
    Bru.   Dismiss them home.
                         [*Exit Ædile.*]

Here comes his mother.

Enter Volumnia, Virgilia, and Menenius.

    Sic.   Let's not meet her.
    Bru.   Why? 8
    Sic. They say she's mad.
    Bru. They have ta'en note of us: keep on your way.
    Vol. O! y' are well met.   The hoarded plague o' the
    gods
Requite your love!

2 have sided: *to have enlisted themselves*
11 The hoarded . . . gods: *every plague the gods have stored up*

Men.   Peace, peace! be not so loud.   12
Vol. If that I could for weeping, you should hear,—
Nay, and you shall hear some. [*To Brutus.*] Will you
    be gone?
Vir. [*To Sicinius.*] You shall stay too.   I would I
    had the power
To say so to my husband.
Sic.   Are you mankind?   16
Vol. Ay, fool; is that a shame?   Note but this fool.
Was not a man my father?   Hadst thou foxship
To banish him that strook more blows for Rome
Than thou hast spoken words?
Sic.   O blessed heavens! 20
Vol. More noble blows than ever thou wise words;
And for Rome's good.   I'll tell thee what; yet go:
Nay, but thou shalt stay too: I would my son
Were in Arabia, and thy tribe before him,   24
His good sword in his hand.
Sic.   What then?
Vir.   What then!
He'd make an end of thy posterity.
Vol. Bastards and all.
Good man, the wounds that he does bear for Rome! 28
Men. Come, come: peace!
Sic. I would he had continu'd to his country
As he began, and not unknit himself
The noble knot he made.
Bru.   I would he had.   32
Vol. 'I would he had!'   'Twas you incens'd the
    rabble:
Cats, that can judge as fitly of his worth

14 some: *a part*
16 say so: *i.e. command his presence*   mankind: *savage; cf. n.*
18 foxship: *foxlike cunning*   19 strook: *struck*
22 what: *something*   24 Arabia: *the Arabian desert*
32 noble knot: *i.e. bond of faithful service*

As I can of those mysteries which heaven
Will not have earth to know.

   Bru.   Pray, let's go.   36

   Vol. Now, pray, sir, get you gone:
You have done a brave deed.   Ere you go, hear this:
As far as doth the Capitol exceed
The meanest house in Rome, so far my son,—   40
This lady's husband here, this, do you see,—
Whom you have banish'd, does exceed you all.

   Bru. Well, well, we'll leave you.

   Sic.   Why stay we to be baited
With one that wants her wits?

                               Exeunt Tribunes.

   Vol.   Take my prayers with you. 44
I would the gods had nothing else to do
But to confirm my curses!   Could I meet 'em
But once a day, it would unclog my heart
Of what lies heavy to 't.

   Men.   You have told them home, 48
And, by my troth, you have cause.   You'll sup with
   me?

   Vol. Anger's my meat; I sup upon myself,
And so shall starve with feeding.   Come, let's go.
Leave this faint puling and lament as I do,   52
In anger, Juno-like.   Come, come, come.

               Exeunt [*Volumnia and Virgilia*].

   Men. Fie, fie, fie!   *Exit.*

44 With: *by*   46 confirm: *note down for execution*
48 told . . . home: *said all there is to say*
52 faint puling: *weak whining; cf. n.*

Scene Three

[A Highway between Rome and Antium]

Enter a Roman and a Volsce.

Rom. I know you well, sir, and you know me:
your name I think is Adrian.

Vols. It is so, sir: truly, I have forgot you.

Rom. I am a Roman; and my services are, as 4
you are, against 'em: know you me yet?

Vols. Nicanor? No.

Rom. The same, sir.

Vols. You had more beard, when I last saw 8
you; but your favour is well appeared by your
tongue. What's the news in Rome? I have a
note from the Volscian state to find you out there:
you have well saved me a day's journey. 12

Rom. There hath been in Rome strange insur-
rections: the people against the senators, patricians, and nobles.

Vols. Hath been! Is it ended then? Our state 16
thinks not so; they are in a most warlike preparation, and hope to come upon them in the heat of
their division.

Rom. The main blaze of it is past, but a small 20
thing would make it flame again. For the nobles
receive so to heart the banishment of that worthy
Coriolanus, that they are in a ripe aptness to
take all power from the people and to pluck 24
from them their tribunes for ever. This lies
glowing, I can tell you, and is almost mature for
the violent breaking out.

9 favour: *face*   appeared: *made to appear, manifested*
11 note: *instruction*   23 ripe aptness: *complete readiness*
26 glowing: *i.e. like a spark*

Vols. Coriolanus banished!   28

Rom. Banished, sir.

Vols. You will be welcome with this intelligence, Nicanor.

Rom. The day serves well for them now. I 32
have heard it said, the fittest time to corrupt a
man's wife is when she's fallen out with her
husband. Your noble Tullus Aufidius will
appear well in these wars, his great opposer, 36
Coriolanus, being now in no request of his
country.

Vols. He cannot choose. I am most fortunate, thus accidentally to encounter you: you 40
have ended my business, and I will merrily
accompany you home.

Rom. I shall, between this and supper, tell
you most strange things from Rome; all tending 44
to the good of their adversaries. Have you an
army ready, say you?

Vols. A most royal one: the centurions and
their charges distinctly billeted, already in th' 48
entertainment, and to be on foot at an hour's
warning.

Rom. I am joyful to hear of their readiness,
and am the man, I think, that shall set them in 52
present action. So, sir, heartily well met, and
most glad of your company.

Vols. You take my part from me, sir; I have
the most cause to be glad of yours.   56

Rom. Well, let us go together.   *Exeunt.*

32 The day: *the state of affairs*   37 in no request of: *unvalued by*
39 cannot choose: *cannot fail to appear well*
48 distinctly billeted: *carefully enrolled*
49 entertainment: *receipt of pay*   on foot: *under arms*
55 my part: *the words I should say*

Scene Four

[Antium.   Before Aufidius' House]

Enter Coriolanus, in mean apparel, disguised and muffled.

Cor. A goodly city is this Antium.   City,
'Tis I that made thy widows: many an heir
Of these fair edifices 'fore my wars
Have I heard groan and drop: then, know me not,   4
Lest that thy wives with spits and boys with stones
In puny battle slay me.

Enter a Citizen.

Save you, sir.

Cit. And you.
Cor.   Direct me, if it be your will,
Where great Aufidius lies.   Is he in Antium?   8
Cit. He is, and feasts the nobles of the state
At his house this night.
Cor.   Which is his house, beseech you?
Cit. This, here before you.
Cor.   Thank you, sir.   Farewell.
                                        Exit Citizen.
O world, thy slippery turns!   Friends now fast
      sworn,   12
Whose double bosoms seems to wear one heart,
Whose hours, whose bed, whose meal, and exercise,
Are still together, who twin, as 'twere, in love
Unseparable, shall within this hour,   16
On a dissension of a doit, break out

3 'fore my wars: *confronting me in battle*   6 Save: *God preserve*
8 lies: *lodges*   12 thy . . . turns: *how inconstant you are*
13 bosoms seems; *cf. n.*   15 twin: *are joined like twins*
17 dissension . . . doit: *dispute over the value of half a farthing*

To bitterest enmity: so, fellest foes,
Whose passions and whose plots have broke their sleep
To take the one the other, by some chance,   20
Some trick not worth an egg, shall grow dear friends
And interjoin their issues.   So with me:
My birth-place hate I, and my love's upon
This enemy town.   I'll enter: if he slay me,   24
He does fair justice; if he give me way,
I'll do his country service.   *Exit.*

Scene Five

[The Same.   A Hall in Aufidius' House]

Music plays.   Enter a Servingman.

1. Serv. Wine, wine, wine!   What service is
here!   I think our fellows are asleep.   *[Exit.]*

Enter another Servingman.

2. Serv. Where's Cotus? my master calls for
him.   Cotus!   *Exit.* 4

Enter Coriolanus.

Cor. A goodly house: the feast smells well; but I
Appear not like a guest.

Enter the First Servingman.

1. Serv. What would you have, friend?   Whence
are you?   Here's no place for you: pray, go to 8
the door.   *Exit.*

Cor. I have deserv'd no better entertainment,
In being Coriolanus.

18 fellest: *fiercest*   19 passions: *violent emotions*
20 To take . . . other; *cf. n.*
22 interjoin their issues: *intermarry their children (to make the league
     perpetual)*   23 hate; *cf. n.*   25 way: *scope, opportunity*

Enter Second Servant.

2. Serv. Whence are you, sir? Has the porter 12
his eyes in his head, that he gives entrance to
such companions? Pray, get you out.

Cor. Away!

2. Serv. 'Away!' Get you away.   16

Cor. Now, th' art troublesome.

2. Serv. Are you so brave? I'll have you talked
with anon.

Enter Third Servingman. The first meets him.

3. Serv. What fellow's this?   20

1. Serv. A strange one as ever I looked on: I
cannot get him out o' the house: prithee, call my
master to him.

3. Serv. What have you to do here, fellow? 24
Pray you, avoid the house.

Cor. Let me but stand; I will not hurt your
hearth.

3. Serv. What are you?   28

Cor. A gentleman.

3. Serv. A marvellous poor one.

Cor. True, so I am.

3. Serv. Pray you, poor gentleman, take up 32
some other station; here's no place for you; pray
you, avoid: come.

Cor. Follow your function; go, and batten on
cold bits.   *Pushes him away from him.* 36

3. Serv. What, you will not? Prithee, tell
my master what a strange guest he has here.

2. Serv. And I shall. *Exit Second Servingman.*

3. Serv. Where dwell'st thou?   40

14 companions: *rascals*   25 avoid: *get out of*
35 Follow . . . function: *do your proper business*   batten: *fatten*
yourself

Cor. Under the canopy.

3. Serv. 'Under the canopy!'

Cor. Ay.

3. Serv. Where's that?   44

Cor. I' the city of kites and crows.

3. Serv. 'I' the city of kites and crows!' What
an ass it is!   Then thou dwell'st with daws
too?   48

Cor. No; I serve not thy master.

3. Serv. How sir!   Do you meddle with my
master?

Cor. Ay; 'tis an honester service than to 52
meddle with thy mistress.
Thou prat'st, and prat'st: serve with thy trencher.
   Hence.   *Beats him away.*

Enter Aufidius with the .[*Second*] *Servingman.*

Auf. Where is this fellow?

2. Serv. Here, sir: I'd have beaten him like a 56
dog, but for disturbing the lords within.

Auf. Whence com'st thou? what wouldst thou?   Thy
   name?
Why speak'st not?   Speak, man: what's thy name?

Cor. [*Unmuffling.*] If, Tullus,   60
Not yet thou know'st me, and, seeing me, dost not
Think me for the man I am, necessity
Commands me name myself.

Auf.   What is thy name?

Cor. A name unmusical to the Volscians' ears,   64
And harsh in sound to thine.

Auf.   Say, what's thy name?
Thou hast a grim appearance, and thy face
Bears a command in 't; though thy tackle's torn,

41 canopy: *sky*   47 daws: *jackdaws, fools*
54 trencher: *wooden platter*   67 tackle: *rigging of ship*

Thou show'st a noble vessel. What's thy name?   68
  Cor. Prepare thy brow to frown. Know'st thou
    me yet?
  Auf. I know thee not. Thy name?
  Cor. My name is Caius Martius, who hath done
To thee particularly, and to all the Volsces,   72
Great hurt and mischief; thereto witness may
My surname, Coriolanus: the painful service,
The extreme dangers, and the drops of blood
Shed for my thankless country are requited   76
But with that surname; a good memory
And witness of the malice and displeasure
Which thou shouldst bear me: only that name remains;
The cruelty and envy of the people,   80
Permitted by our dastard nobles, who
Have all forsook me, hath devour'd the rest;
And suffer'd me by the voice of slaves to be
Whoop'd out of Rome. Now this extremity   84
Hath brought me to thy hearth; not out of hope,—
Mistake me not,—to save my life; for if
I had fear'd death, of all the men i' the world
I would have 'voided thee; but in mere spite,   88
To be full quit of those my banishers,
Stand I before thee here. Then if thou hast
A heart of wreak in thee, that will revenge
Thine own particular wrongs and stop those maims 92
Of shame seen through thy country, speed thee
    straight,
And make my misery serve thy turn: so use it,
That my revengeful services may prove
As benefits to thee, for I will fight   96

77 memory: *reminder*   84 Whoop'd: *hooted*
89 full quit of: *fully avenged on*
91 heart of wreak: *vengeful heart*
92, 93 maims . . . shame: *disgraceful losses of men or territory*

Against my canker'd country with the spleen
Of all the under fiends.   But if so be
Thou dar'st not this, and that to prove more fortunes
Th' art tir'd, then, in a word, I also am   100
Longer to live most weary, and present
My throat to thee and to thy ancient malice;
Which not to cut would show thee but a fool,
Since I have ever follow'd thee with hate,   104
Drawn tuns of blood out of thy country's breast,
And cannot live but to thy shame, unless
It be to do thee service.
   Auf.   O Martius, Martius!
Each word thou hast spoke hath weeded from my
     heart   108
A root of ancient envy.   If Jupiter
Should from yond cloud speak divine things,
And·say, ''Tis true,' I'd not believe them more
Than thee, all noble Martius.   Let me twine   112
Mine arms about that body, where against
My grained ash an hundred times hath broke,
And scarr'd the moon with splinters: here I clip
The anvil of my sword, and do contest   116
As hotly and as nobly with thy love
As ever in ambitious strength I did
Contend against thy valour.   Know thou first,
I lov'd the maid I married; never man   120
Sigh'd truer breath; but that I see thee here,
Thou noble thing! more dances my rapt heart
Than when I first my wedded mistress saw

97 canker'd: *malevolent*   spleen: *anger*
99 prove . . . fortunes: *try your fortune further*
105 tuns: *huge barrels*
109 A root . . . envy: *one of the old sources of my hate*
113 where against: *against which*
114 grained ash: *spear-shaft of tough ash*   115 clip: *embrace*
121 Sigh'd . . . breath: *uttered sincerer love sighs*
122 dances: *makes leap*   rapt: *enraptured*

Bestride my threshold. Why, thou Mars! I tell
   thee,   124
We have a power on foot; and I had purpose
Once more to hew thy target from thy brawn,
Or lose mine arm for 't. Thou hast beat me out
Twelve several times, and I have nightly since   128
Dreamt of encounters 'twixt thyself and me;
We have been down together in my sleep,
Unbuckling helms, fisting each other's throat,   131
And wak'd half dead with nothing. Worthy Martius,
Had we no quarrel else to Rome, but that
Thou art thence banish'd, we would muster all
From twelve to seventy, and, pouring war
Into the bowels of ungrateful Rome,   136
Like a bold flood o'er-bear. O! come; go in,
And take our friendly senators by the hands,
Who now are here, taking their leaves of me,
Who am prepar'd against your territories,   140
Though not for Rome itself.

    Cor.   You bless me, gods!

    Auf. Therefore, most absolute sir, if thou wilt have
The leading of thine own revenges, take
Th' one half of my commission, and set down,   144
As best thou art experienc'd, since thou know'st
Thy country's strength and weakness, thine own ways;
Whether to knock against the gates of Rome,
Or rudely visit them in parts remote,   148
To fright them, ere destroy. But come in:
Let me commend thee first to those that shall
Say yea to thy desires. A thousand welcomes!
And more a friend than e'er an enemy;   152

126 brawn: *brawny arm*   127 out: *outright*
132 wak'd: *I have awaked*
137 o'er-bear: *bear all before us; cf. n.*
142 absolute: *perfect*   144 set down: *determine*

Yet, Martius, that was much.   Your hand: most welcome!   *Exeunt.*

         Enter two of the Servingmen.

   1. Serv. Here's a strange alteration!

   2. Serv. By my hand, I had thought to 156
have strucken him with a cudgel; and yet my
mind gave me his clothes made a false report of
him.

   1. Serv. What an arm he has! He turned me 160
about with his finger and his thumb, as one would
set up a top.

   2. Serv. Nay, I knew by his face that there
was something in him: he had, sir, a kind of face, 164
methought,—I cannot tell how to term it.

   1. Serv. He had so; looking as it were,—would
I were hanged but I thought there was more in
him than I could think.   168

   2. Serv. So did I, I'll be sworn: he is simply
the rarest man i' the world.

   1. Serv. I think he is; but a greater soldier
than he you wot on.   172

   2. Serv. Who? my master?

   1. Serv. Nay, it's no matter for that.

   2. Serv. Worth six on him.

   1. Serv. Nay, not so neither; but I take him 176
to be the greater soldier.

   2. Serv. Faith, look you, one cannot tell how
to say that: for the defence of a town our general
is excellent.   180

   1. Serv. Ay, and for an assault too.

153 S. d. Enter . . . Servingmen; *cf. n.*
158 gave me: *misgave me, made me suspect*
162 set up: *start spinning*
172 he . . . on: *the man you know of, i.e. Aufidius; cf. n.*

Enter the Third Servingman.

3. Serv. O slaves! I can tell you news; news,
you rascals.

Both. What, what, what? let's partake.   184

3. Serv. I would not be a Roman, of all nations;
I had as lief be a condemned man.

Both. Wherefore? wherefore?

3. Serv. Why, here's he that was wont to 188
thwack our general, Caius Martius.

1. Serv. Why do you say 'thwack our
general?'

3. Serv. I do not say, 'thwack our general'; 192
but he was always good enough for him.

2. Serv. Come, we are fellows and friends: he
was ever too hard for him; I have heard him say
so himself.   196

1. Serv. He was too hard for him,—directly
to say the truth on 't: before Corioli he scotched
him and notched him like a carbonado.

2. Serv. An he had been cannibally given, he 200
might have boiled and eaten him too.

1. Serv. But, more of thy news.

3. Serv. Why, he is so made on here
within, as if he were son and heir to Mars; set 204
at upper end o' the table; no question asked
him by any of the senators, but they stand bald
before him. Our general himself makes a mistress
of him; sanctifies himself with 's hand, and turns 208
up the white o' th' eye to his discourse. But the

184 let's partake: *let us share it*
197 directly: *candidly*
199 notched: *cut*   carbonado: *steak prepared for broiling*
201 boiled; *cf. n.*
208 sanctifies . . . hand: *fondles his hand as if it were a saint's relic*
208, 209 turns . . . eye: *gazes upward in reverence*

189 thwack: *beat*
198 scotched: *slashed*
203 made on: *made much of, pampered*

bottom of the news is, our general is cut i' the middle, and but one half of what he was yesterday, for the other has half, by the entreaty and 212 grant of the whole table. He'll go, he says, and sowl the porter of Rome gates by the ears: he will mow down all before him, and leave his passage polled. 216

2. Serv. And he's as like to do 't as any man I can imagine.

3. Serv. Do 't! he will do 't; for—look you, sir—he has as many friends as enemies; which 220 friends, sir—as it were—durst not—look you, sir—show themselves—as we term it—his friends, whilst he's in directitude.

1. Serv. Directitude! what's that? 224

3. Serv. But when they shall see, sir, his crest up again, and the man in blood, they will out of their burrows, like conies after rain, and revel all with him. 228

1. Serv. But when goes this forward?

3. Serv. To-morrow; to-day; presently. You shall have the drum strook up this afternoon; 'tis, as it were, a parcel of their feast, and to be 232 executed ere they wipe their lips.

2. Serv. Why, then we shall have a stirring world again. This peace is nothing but to rust iron, increase tailors, and breed ballad-makers. 236

1. Serv. Let me have war, say I; it exceeds peace as far as day does night; it's spritely,

---

210 bottom: *fundamental part*
212, 213 by . . . table: *the whole table uniting both in requesting and granting*
                                                214 sowl: *drag*
215, 216 leave . . . polled: *leave headless bodies where he passes*
223 directitude: *error for 'discreditude,' discredit(?)*
226 in blood: *in fine fettle*   227 conies: *rabbits*
230 presently: *at once*   232 parcel: *part*
235 nothing: *good for nothing*

waking, audible, and full of vent.　Peace is a
very apoplexy, lethargy; mulled, deaf, sleepy, 240
insensible; a getter of more bastard children than
war's a destroyer of men.

2. Serv. 'Tis so: and as war, in some sort, may
be said to be a ravisher, so it cannot be denied 244
but peace is a great maker of cuckolds.

1. Serv. Ay, and it makes men hate one
another.

3. Serv. Reason: because they then less need 248
one another.　The wars for my money.　I hope
to see Romans as cheap as Volscians.　They are
rising, they are rising.

All. In, in, in, in!　　　　　　　　　*Exeunt.* 252

Scene Six

[*Rome.　A Public Place*]

Enter the two Tribunes, Sicinius and Brutus.

Sic. We hear not of him, neither need we fear him;
His remedies are tame i' the present peace
And quietness o' the people, which before
Were in wild hurry.　Here do we make his friends　4
Blush that the world goes well, who rather had,
Though they themselves did suffer by 't, behold
Dissentious numbers pestering streets, than see
Our tradesmen singing in their shops and going　8
About their functions friendly.

---

239 audible: *noisy(?), quick of hearing(?)*　　　vent: *opportunity for
　　action*　　　240 mulled: *insipid, like warmed and sweetened wine*
241 insensible: *sluggish, insensitive*
248 Reason: *that is natural*　　　251 rising: *getting up from table*
2 remedies: *means of reinstatement*　　　　tame: *languid, ineffectual;*
　　cf. n.　　　　　　　　　　　　　　　　　　4 hurry: *turbulence*
7 pestering: *blocking up*　　　9 friendly: *like good friends*

Enter Menenius.

Bru. We stood to 't in good time.   Is this Menenius?
Sic. 'Tis he, 'tis he.   O! he is grown most kind
Of late.   Hail, sir!
    Men.   Hail to you both!   12
    Sic. Your Coriolanus is not much miss'd
But with his friends: the commonwealth doth stand,
And so would do, were he more angry at it.
    Men. All's well; and might have been much better,
      if   16
He could have temporiz'd.
    Sic.   Where is he, hear you?
    Men. Nay, I hear nothing: his mother and his wife
Hear nothing from him.

Enter three or four Citizens.

    All. The gods preserve you both!
    Sic.   Good den, our neighbours. 20
    Bru. Good den to you all, good den to you all.
    1. Cit. Ourselves, our wives, and children, on our
      knees,
Are bound to pray for you both.
    Sic.   Live, and thrive!
    Bru. Farewell, kind neighbours: we wish'd Corio-
      lanus   24
Had lov'd you as we did.
    All.   Now the gods keep you!
    Both Tri. Farewell, farewell.   *Exeunt Citizens.*
    Sic. This is a happier and more comely time
Than when these fellows ran about the streets   28
Crying confusion.
    Bru.   Caius Martius was

14 But with: *except among*   27 comely: *gracious*
29 Crying confusion: *shouting for anarchy*

A worthy officer i' the war; but insolent,
O'ercome with pride, ambitious past all thinking,
Self-loving,—

Sic.   And affecting one sole throne,   32
Without assistance.

Men.   I think not so.

Sic. We should by this, to all our lamentation,
If he had gone forth consul, found it so.

Bru. The gods have well prevented it, and Rome   36
Sits safe and still without him.

Enter an Ædile.

Æd.   Worthy tribunes,
There is a slave, whom we have put in prison,
Reports, the Volsces with two several powers
Are enter'd in the Roman territories,   40
And with the deepest malice of the war
Destroy what lies before 'em.

Men.   'Tis Aufidius,
Who, hearing of our Martius' banishment,
Thrusts forth his horns again into the world;   44
Which were inshell'd when Martius stood for Rome,
And durst not once peep out.

Sic. Come, what talk you of Martius?

Bru. Go see this rumourer whipp'd. It cannot be 48
The Volsces dare break with us.

Men.   Cannot be!
We have record that very well it can,
And three examples of the like hath been
Within my age. But reason with the fellow,   52

32 affecting . . . throne: *aiming at individual sovereignty*
34 by this: *by this time*   to . . . lamentation: *to the sorrow of us all*
35 gone forth: *come out, finally become*   found: *have found*
44 Thrusts . . . horns; *cf. n.*
45 inshell'd: *drawn within the shell*   stood for: *was champion of*
47 what: *why*

Before you punish him, where he heard this,
Lest you shall chance to whip your information,
And beat the messenger who bids beware
Of what is to be dreaded.

 Sic.   Tell not me: 56
I know this cannot be.

 Bru.   Not possible.

Enter a Messenger.

 Mess. The nobles in great earnestness are going
All to the senate-house: some news is coming,
That turns their countenances.

 Sic.   'Tis this slave.— 60
Go whip him 'fore the people's eyes: his raising;
Nothing but his report.

 Mess.   Yes, worthy sir,
The slave's report is seconded; and more,
More fearful, is deliver'd.

 Sic.   What more fearful? 64

 Mess. It is spoke freely out of many mouths—
How probable I do not know—that Martius,
Join'd with Aufidius, leads a power 'gainst Rome,
And vows revenge as spacious as between 68
The young'st and oldest thing.

 Sic.   This is most likely!

 Bru. Rais'd only, that the weaker sort may wish
Good Martius home again.

 Sic.   The very trick on 't.

 Men. This is unlikely: 72
He and Aufidius can no more atone
Than violent'st contrariety.

Enter [another] Messenger.

59 coming; *cf. n.*   68, 69 And vows . . . thing; *cf. n.*
73 atone: *grow reconciled*

Mess. You are sent for to the senate:
A fearful army, led by Caius Martius,   76
Associated with Aufidius, rages
Upon our territories; and have already
O'erborne their way, consum'd with fire, and took
What lay before them.   80

Enter Cominius.

Com. O! you have made good work!
Men.   What news? what news?
Com. You have holp to ravish your own daughters, and
To melt the city leads upon your pates,
To see your wives dishonour'd to your noses,—   84
Men. What's the news? what's the news?
Com. Your temples burned in their cement, and
Your franchises, whereon you stood, confin'd
Into an auger's bore.
Men.   Pray now, your news?—   88
You have made fair work, I fear me. Pray, your news?
If Martius should be join'd with Volscians,—
Com.   If!
He is their god: he leads them like a thing
Made by some other deity than Nature,   92
That shapes man better; and they follow him,
Against us brats, with no less confidence
Than boys pursuing summer butterflies,
Or butchers killing flies.
Men.   You have made good work, 96
You, and your apron-men; you that stood so much

79 O'erborne . . . way: *advanced like a wave*   82 holp: *helped*
83 leads: *leaden roofs*   84 to: *before*
86 temples . . . cement; *cf. n.*
87 franchises: *public rights*   whereon . . . stood: *which you
    asserted*   87, 88 confin'd . . . bore: *reduced to absolute nullity*
94 brats: *mere children*   97 apron-men: *artisans, dressed in aprons*

Upon the voice of occupation and
The breath of garlic-eaters!

Com.   He'll shake
Your Rome about your ears.

Men.   As Hercules   100
Did shake down mellow fruit.   You have made **fair
    work**!

Bru. But is this true, sir?

Com.   Ay; and you'll look pale
Before you find it other.   All the regions
Do smilingly revolt; and who resist   104
Are mock'd for valiant ignorance,
And perish constant fools.   Who is 't can blame him?
Your enemies, and his, find something in him.

Men. We are all undone unless   108
The noble man have mercy.

Com.   Who shall ask it?
The tribunes cannot do 't for shame; the people
Deserve such pity of him as the wolf
Does of the shepherds: for his best friends, if they   112
Should say, 'Be good to Rome,' they charg'd him even
As those should do that had deserv'd his hate,
And therein show'd like enemies.

Men.   'Tis true:
If he were putting to my house the brand   116
That should consume it, I have not the face
To say, 'Beseech you, cease.'—You have made **fair
    hands**,
You and your crafts! you have crafted fair!

Com.   You have brought
A trembling upon Rome, such as was never   120

98 voice of occupation: *workmen's opinion*   103 other: *otherwise*
104 smilingly: *gladly*   who resist: *those who resist*
113 charg'd: *would be urging; cf. n.*   115 show'd: *would appear*
118 made fair hands: *done fine work*
119 crafted; *cf. n.*   fair: *with beautiful results*

So incapable of help.
   Tribunes.   Say not we brought it.
   Men. How! Was 't we? We lov'd him; but, like beasts
And cowardly nobles, gave way unto your clusters,
Who did hoot him out o' the city.
   Com.   But I fear   124
They'll roar him in again. Tullus Aufidius,
The second name of men, obeys his points
As if he were his officer: desperation
Is all the policy, strength, and defence,   128
That Rome can make against them.

Enter a troop of Citizens.

   Men.   Here come the clusters.
And is Aufidius with him? You are they
That made the air unwholesome, when you cast
Your stinking greasy caps in hooting at   132
Coriolanus' exile. Now he's coming;
And not a hair upon a soldier's head
Which will not prove a whip: as many coxcombs
As you threw caps up will he tumble down,   136
And pay you for your voices. 'Tis no matter;
If he could burn us all into one coal,
We have deserv'd it.
   Omnes. Faith, we hear fearful news.
   1. Cit.   For mine own part, 140
When I said banish him, I said 'twas pity.
   2. Cit. And so did I.
   3. Cit. And so did I; and, to say the

123 clusters: *crowds*
125 roar . . . again: *yell with pain as he returns*
126 second . . . men: *the most famous man except Coriolanus*
    points: *instructions*
127-129 desperation . . . against them; *cf. n.*
135 coxcombs: *fools' heads*   138 coal: *hot ember*

truth, so did very many of us.   That we did we 144
did for the best; and though we willingly con-
sented to his banishment, yet it was against our
will.

Com. Y' are goodly things, you voices!

Men.   You have made 148
Good work, you and your cry! Shall 's to the Capitol?

Com. O! ay; what else?   *Exeunt both.*

Sic. Go, masters, get you home; be not dismay'd:
These are a side that would be glad to have   152
This true which they so seem to fear. Go home,
And show no sign of fear.

1..Cit. The gods be good to us! Come, masters,
let's home. I ever said we were i' the wrong 156
when we banished him.

2. Cit. So did we all. But come, let's home.

                              Exeunt Citizens.

Bru. I do not like this news.

Sic. Nor I.   160

Bru. Let's to the Capitol. Would half my wealth
Would buy this for a lie!

Sic.   Pray let us go.

                              Exeunt Tribunes.

Scene Seven

[*A Camp at a small distance from Rome*]

Enter Aufidius with his Lieutenant.

Auf. Do they still fly to the Roman?

Lieu. I do not know what witchcraft's in him, but
Your soldiers use him as the grace 'fore meat,

149 cry: *pack (of hounds)*   Shall 's: *shall we*
152 a side: *members of a party (i.e. patricians)*

Their talk at table, and their thanks at end;   4
And you are darken'd in this action, sir,
Even by your own.
     Auf.   I cannot help it now,
Unless, by using means, I lame the foot
Of our design. He bears himself more proudlier,   8
Even to my person, than I thought he would
When first I did embrace him; yet his nature
In that's no changeling, and I must excuse
What cannot be amended.
     Lieu.   Yet, I wish, sir,—   12
I mean for your particular,—you had not
Join'd in commission with him; but either
Had borne the action of yourself, or else
To him had left it solely.   16
     Auf. I understand thee well; and be thou sure,
When he shall come to his account, he knows not
What I can urge against him. Although it seems,
And so he thinks, and is no less apparent   20
To the vulgar eye, that he bears all things fairly,
And shows good husbandry for the Volscian state,
Fights dragon-like, and does achieve as soon
As draw his sword; yet he hath left undone   24
That which shall break his neck or hazard mine,
Whene'er we come to our account.
     Lieu. Sir, I beseech you, think you he'll carry
       Rome?
     Auf. All places yields to him ere he sits down;   28

5 darken'd: *dimmed in glory*   action: *campaign*
6 your own: *your own troops*   7 using means: *employing treachery*
11 no changeling: *i.e. still what it always was*
13 particular: *personal advantage*   14 commission: *authority*
15 borne . . . yourself: *taken the whole command yourself*
21 bears . . . fairly: *behaves honorably in all respects*
23 achieve: *conquer*   24-26 yet . . . account; *cf. n.*
27 carry: *take by force*   28 sits down: *besieges*

And the nobility of Rome are his:
The senators and patricians love him too:
The tribunes are no soldiers; and their people
Will be as rash in the repeal as hasty   32
To expel him thence.   I think he'll be to Rome
As is the osprey to the fish, who takes it
By sovereignty of nature.   First he was
A noble servant to them, but he could not   36
Carry his honours even; whether 'twas pride,
Which out of daily fortune ever taints
The happy man; whether defect of judgment,
To fail in the disposing of those chances   40
Which he was lord of; or whether nature,
Not to be other than one thing, not moving
From the casque to the cushion, but commanding peace
Even with the same austerity and garb   44
As he controll'd the war; but one of these,
As he hath spices of them all, not all,
For I dare so far free him, made him fear'd,
So hated, and so banish'd: but he has a merit   48
To choke it in the utterance.   So our virtues
Lie in th' interpretation of the time;
And power, unto itself most commendable,
Hath not a tomb so evident as a chair   52
To extol what it hath done.
One fire drives out one fire; one nail, one nail;
Rights by rights falter, strengths by strengths do fail.

34, 35 osprey . . . nature; *cf. n.*   37 even: *steadily*
38 out . . . fortune: *as a result of constant good fortune*   taints:
    sullies   40 disposing: *exploiting*
42 Not to be: *not capable of being*
42, 43 not moving . . . cushion; *cf. n.*
44 austerity and garb: *austere manner*
46 spices . . . not all: *some flavor of all these faults, but not in full
    degree*   47 free: *acquit*
48 So: *and therefore (i.e. because feared)*
48, 49 but . . . utterance; *cf. n.*   50 Lie in: *depend upon*
51-53 *Cf. n.*   55 Rights . . . falter; *cf. n.*

Come, let's away. When, Caius, Rome is thine,   56
Thou art poor'st of all; then shortly art thou mine.

                             Exeunt.

ACT FIFTH

Scene One

[*Rome. A Public Place*]

*Enter Menenius, Cominius, Sicinius, Brutus (the two
Tribunes), with Others.*

  Men. No, I'll not go: you hear what he hath said
Which was sometime his general; who lov'd him
In a most dear particular. He call'd me father:
But what o' that? Go, you that banish'd him;   4
A mile before his tent fall down, and knee
The way into his mercy. Nay, if he coy'd
To hear Cominius speak, I'll keep at home.
  Com. He would not seem to know me.
  Men.   Do you hear? 8
  Com. Yet one time he did call me by my name.
I urg'd our old acquaintance, and the drops
That we have bled together. Coriolanus
He would not answer to; forbad all names;   12
He was a kind of nothing, titleless,
Till he had forg'd himself a name o' the fire
Of burning Rome.
  Men.   Why, so: you have made good work!
A pair of tribunes that have rack'd for Rome,   16
To make coals cheap: a noble memory!

---

3 particular: *personal relation*   5 knee: *crawl on your knees*
6 coy'd: *held back, showed reluctance*
12 forbad: *prohibited the use of*   14 o': *out of*
16 rack'd: *strained themselves, worked desperately; cf. n.*
17 coals: *cinders, charcoal*

Com. I minded him how royal 'twas to pardon
When it was less expected: he replied,
It was a bare petition of a state   20
To one whom they had punish'd.

Men.   Very well.
Could he say less?

Com. I offer'd to awaken his regard
For 's private friends: his answer to me was,   24
He could not stay to pick them in a pile
Of noisome musty chaff: he said 'twas folly,
For one poor grain or two, to leave unburnt
And still to nose th' offence.

Men.   For one poor grain or two! 28
I am one of those; his mother, wife, his child,
And this brave fellow too, we are the grains:
You are the musty chaff, and you are smelt
Above the moon.   We must be burnt for you.   32

Sic. Nay, pray, be patient: if you refuse your aid
In this so-never-needed help, yet do not
Upbraid 's with our distress.   But, sure, if you
Would be your country's pleader, your good tongue, 36
More than the instant army we can make,
Might stop our countryman.

Men.   No; I'll not meddle.

Sic. Pray you, go to him.

Men. What should I do?   40

Bru. Only make trial what your love can do
For Rome towards Martius.

Men.   Well; and say that Martius
Return me, as Cominius is return'd,

18 minded: *reminded*   20 bare: *threadbare, poor*
23 offer'd: *presumed*
28 nose: *smell*   offence: *nuisance, offensive matter*
37 instant: *capable of being raised at once*
42 towards: *in relation to*

Unheard; what then?   44
But as a discontented friend, grief-shot
With his unkindness? say 't be so?

Sic.   Yet your good will
Must have that thanks from Rome, after the measure
As you intended well.

Men.   I'll undertake 't: 48
I think he'll hear me.   Yet, to bite his lip,
And hum at good Cominius, much unhearts me.
He was not taken well; he had not din'd:
The veins unfill'd, our blood is cold, and then   52
We pout upon the morning, are unapt
To give or to forgive; but when we have stuff'd
These pipes and these conveyances of our blood
With wine and feeding, we have suppler souls   56
Than in our priestlike fasts: therefore, I'll watch him
Till he be dieted to my request,
And then I'll set upon him.

Bru. You know the very road into his kindness,   60
And cannot lose your way.

Men.   Good faith, I'll prove him,
Speed how it will.   I shall ere long have knowledge
Of my success.   *Exit.*

Com.   He'll never hear him.

Sic.   Not?

Com. I tell you he does sit in gold, his eye   64
Red as 'twould burn Rome, and his injury
The gaoler to his pity.   I kneel'd before him;
'Twas very faintly he said 'Rise'; dismiss'd me

45 grief-shot: *pierced with grief*
47, 48 after . . . well: *proportionate to the goodness of your intention*
50 unhearts: *dispirits*   51 taken well: *propitiously encountered*
58 dieted to: *fed up auspiciously for*   62 Speed: *turn out*
63 Of . . . success: *how I shall fare*
64 in gold: *on golden throne*   67 faintly: *coldly*

Thus, with his speechless hand: what he would do   68
He sent in writing after me, what he would not,
Bound with an oath to yield to his conditions:
So that all hope is vain
Unless his noble mother and his wife,   72
Who, as I hear, mean to solicit him
For mercy to his country. Therefore let's hence,
And with our fair entreaties haste them on.   *Exeunt.*

Scene Two

[*The Volscian Camp before Rome. The Guards at their stations*]

Enter Menenius to the Watch or Guard.

1. Wat. Stay! whence are you?

2. Wat.   Stand! and go back.

Men. You guard like men; 'tis well; but, by your leave,
I am an officer of state, and come
To speak with Coriolanus.

1. Wat.   From whence?

Men.   From Rome. 4

1. Wat. You may not pass; you must return: our general
Will no more hear from thence.

2. Wat. You'll see your Rome embrac'd with fire before
You'll speak with Coriolanus.

Men.   Good my friends, 8
If you have heard your general talk of Rome,
And of his friends there, it is lots to blanks

68-70 what . . . conditions; *cf. n.*
72 Unless: *unless in the efforts of*
        10 lots to blanks; *cf. n.*

My name hath touch'd your ears: it is Menenius.

1. Wat. Be it so; go back: the virtue of your name 12
Is not here passable.

Men.   I tell thee, fellow,
Thy general is my lover: I have been
The book of his good acts, whence men have read
His fame unparallel'd, haply amplified;   16
For I have ever verified my friends—
Of whom he's chief—with all the size that verity
Would without lapsing suffer: nay, sometimes,
Like to a bowl upon a subtle ground,   20
I have tumbled past the throw, and in his praise
Have almost stamp'd the leasing.   Therefore, fellow,
I must have leave to pass.

1. Wat. Faith, sir, if you had told as many 24
lies in his behalf as you have uttered words in
your own, you should not pass here; no, though
it were as virtuous to lie as to live chastely.
Therefore go back.   28

Men. Prithee, fellow, remember my name is
Menenius, always factionary on the party of your
general.

2. Wat. Howsoever you have been his liar 32
— as you say you have — I am one that,
telling true under him, must say you cannot pass.
Therefore go back.

Men. Has he dined, canst thou tell? for I 36
would not speak with him till after dinner.

1. Wat. You are a Roman, are you?

Men. I am as thy general is.

13 passable: *valid*   15 book: *record, that which reports*
17 verified my friends: *shown my friends to be my friends; cf. n.*
18 size: *exaggeration*   19 lapsing: *slipping into falsehood*
20 subtle: *temptingly level*   21 throw: *distance aimed at*
22 stamp'd the leasing: *confirmed actual falsehood*
30 factionary . . . party: *an active adherent*
34 telling . . . him: *speaking truth in his service*

1. Wat. Then you should hate Rome, as he 40
does.   Can you, when you have pushed out
your gates the very defender of them, and, in a
violent popular ignorance, given your enemy
your shield, think to front his revenges with the 44
easy groans of old women, the virginal palms of
your daughters, or with the palsied intercession
of such a decayed dotant as you seem to be?
Can you think to blow out the intended fire your 48
city is ready to flame in with such weak breath
as this?   No, you are deceived; therefore, back
to Rome, and prepare for your execution: you
are condemned, our general has sworn you out 52
of reprieve and pardon.

Men. Sirrah, if thy captain knew I were here,
he would use me with estimation.

1. Wat. Come, my captain knows you not.   56

Men. I mean, thy general.

1. Wat. My general cares not for you.
Back, I say: go, lest I let forth your half-pint of
blood; back, that's the utmost of your having: 60
back!

Men. Nay, but, fellow, fellow,—

Enter Coriolanus with Aufidius.

Cor. What's the matter?

Men. Now, you companion, I'll say an errand 64
for you: you shall know now that I am in
estimation; you shall perceive that a Jack
guardant cannot office me from my son Corio-

41 out: *out of*   43 violent . . . ignorance: *folly of mob violence*
44 front: *meet*   47 dotant: *dotard*
52, 53 out of: *beyond the reach of*   55 estimation: *esteem*
60 the utmost . . . having: *the most you shall get*
64, 65 say . . . for you: *make a report about you*
66, 67 Jack guardant: *good-for-nothing sentry*
67 office: *officiously detain*

lanus: guess, but by my entertainment with 68
him, if thou standest not i' the state of hanging,
or of some death more long in spectatorship,
and crueller in suffering; behold now presently,
and swound for what's to come upon thee. [*To* 72
Coriolanus.]   The glorious gods sit in hourly
synod about thy particular prosperity, and love
thee no worse than thy old father Menenius
does! O my son! my son! thou art preparing 76
fire for us; look thee, here's water to quench it.
I was hardly moved to come to thee; but being
assured none but myself could move thee, I
have been blown out of your gates with sighs; 80
and conjure thee to pardon Rome, and thy
petitionary countrymen. The good gods assuage
thy wrath, and turn the dregs of it upon this
varlet here; this, who, like a block, hath denied 84
my access to thee.

   Cor. Away!

   Men. How! away!

Cor. Wife, mother, child, I know not.   My affairs 88
Are servanted to others: though I owe
My revenge properly, my remission lies
In Volscian breasts.   That we have been familiar,
Ingrate forgetfulness shall poison, rather   92
Than pity note how much.   Therefore, begone:
Mine ears against your suits are stronger than
Your gates against my force.   Yet, for I lov'd thee,
Take this along; I writ it for thy sake,   96

                [*Gives a paper.*]

68 entertainment: *reception*
70 more . . . spectatorship: *which will still more prolong your public
ignominy*   72 swound: *swoon*   74 synod: *conference*
80 your: *i.e. the Roman*   84 block: *block of wood, blockhead*
89 servanted: *made servants*
90 properly: *personally*   remission: *forgiveness, mercy; cf. n.*
91-93 That . . . much; *cf. n.*   95 for: *because*

And would have sent it.   Another word, Menenius,
I will not hear thee speak.   This man, Aufidius,
Was my belov'd in Rome: yet thou behold'st!

Auf. You keep a constant temper.   100

> *Exeunt [Coriolanus and Aufidius].*
> *Mane[n]t the Guard and Menenius.*

1. Wat. Now, sir, is your name Menenius?

2. Wat. 'Tis a spell, you see, of much power.
You know the way home again.

1. Wat. Do you hear how we are shent for 104
keeping your greatness back?

2. Wat. What cause, do you think, I have to
swound?

Men. I neither care for the world, nor your 108
general: for such things as you, I can scarce
think there's any, y' are so slight.   He that hath
a will to die by himself fears it not from another.
Let your general do his worst.   For you, be that 112
you are long; and your misery increase with your
age!   I say to you, as I was said to, Away!   *Exit.*

1. Wat. A noble fellow, I warrant him.

2. Wat. The worthy fellow is our general: 116
he's the rock, the oak, not to be wind-shaken.

> *Exit Watch.*

Scene Three

[*The Tent of Coriolanus*]

Enter Coriolanus and Aufidius.

Cor. We will before the walls of Rome to-morrow
Set down our host.   My partner in this action,

---

104 shent: *scolded*   110, 111 He . . . another; *cf. n.*
112, 113 be . . . long: *may you remain long in your present wretched
     state*

You must report to the Volscian lords, how plainly
I have borne this business.

   Auf.   Only their ends   **4**
You have respected; stopp'd your ears against
The general suit of Rome; never admitted
A private whisper; no, not with such friends
That thought them sure of you.

   Cor.   This last old man,   **8**
Whom with a crack'd heart I have sent to Rome,
Lov'd me above the measure of a father;
Nay, godded me indeed.   Their latest refuge
Was to send him; for whose old love I have,   **12**
Though I show'd sourly to him, once more offer'd
The first conditions, which they did refuse,
And cannot now accept, to grace him only
That thought he could do more.   A very little   **16**
I have yielded to; fresh embassies and suits,
Nor from the state, nor private friends, hereafter
Will I lend ear to.   Ha! what shout is this?

                              Shout within.

Shall I be tempted to infringe my vow   **20**
In the same time 'tis made?   I will not.

*Enter Virgilia, Volumnia, Valeria, young Martius,
           with Attendants.*

My wife comes foremost; then the honour'd mould
Wherein this trunk was fram'd, and in her hand
The grandchild to her blood.   But out, affection!   **24**
All bond and privilege of nature, break!
Let it be virtuous to be obstinate.
What is that curtsy worth? or those doves' eyes,
Which can make gods forsworn?   I melt, and am not **28**

3 plainly: *candidly, honestly*   4 borne: *conducted*
6 general . . . Rome: *petitions of all Rome*   11 godded: *deified*
18 Nor . . . friends: *neither from the state nor from private friends*
23 in . . . hand: *led by the hand*

Of stronger earth than others.   My mother bows,
As if Olympus to a molehill should
In supplication nod; and my young boy
Hath an aspect of intercession, which   32
Great nature cries, 'Deny not.'   Let the Volsces
Plough Rome, and harrow Italy; I'll never
Be such a gosling to obey instinct, but stand
As if a man were author of himself   36
And knew no other kin.

    Vir.   My lord and husband!

    Cor. These eyes are not the same I wore in Rome.

    Vir. The sorrow that delivers us thus chang'd
Makes you think so.

    Cor.   Like a dull actor now,   40
I have forgot my part, and I am out,
Even to a full disgrace.   Best of my flesh,
Forgive my tyranny; but do not say
For that, 'Forgive our Romans.'   O! a kiss   44
Long as my exile, sweet as my revenge!
Now, by the jealous queen of heaven, that kiss
I carried from thee, dear, and my true lip
Hath virgin'd it e'er since.   You gods! I prate,   48
And the most noble mother of the world
Leave unsaluted.   Sink, my knee, i' the earth;

                                      Kneels.

Of thy deep duty more impression show
Than that of common sons.

    Vol.   O! stand up bless'd;   52
Whilst, with no softer cushion than the flint,
I kneel before thee, and unproperly

35 gosling: *young goose*
38 These . . . same: *i.e. I look upon you with different feelings*
39 thus chang'd: *in mourning garb; cf. n.*
41 out: *at loss for the proper words*
51 duty: *dutifulness, respect*   more . . . show; *cf. n.*
54 unproperly: *abnormally*

Show duty, as mistaken all this while
Between the child and parent.   [*Kneels.*]
  Cor.   What's this?   56
Your knees to me! to your corrected son!
Then let the pebbles on the hungry beach
Fillip the stars; then let the mutinous winds
Strike the proud cedars 'gainst the fiery sun,   60
Murd'ring impossibility, to make
What cannot be, slight work.
  Vol.   Thou art my warrior;
I holp to frame thee.   Do you know this lady?
  Cor. The noble sister of Publicola,   64
The moon of Rome; chaste as the icicle
That's curdied by the frost from purest snow,
And hangs on Dian's temple: dear Valeria!
  Vol. This is a poor epitome of yours,   68
                  [*Pointing to the Child.*]
Which by th' interpretation of full time
May show like all yourself.
  Cor.   The god of soldiers,
With the consent of supreme Jove, inform
Thy thoughts with nobleness; that thou mayst prove 72
To shame unvulnerable, and stick i' the wars
Like a great sea-mark, standing every flaw,
And saving those that eye thee!
  Vol.   Your knee, sirrah.
  Cor. That's my brave boy!   76
  Vol. Even he, your wife, this lady, and myself

---

55 as mistaken: *as if the obligation of deference had been misunderstood*   57 corrected: *yielding to correction, submissive*
58 hungry: *sterile(?), voracious(?)*   59 Fillip: *hit against*
61 Murd'ring: *annulling*   62 slight work: *a trivial task*
66 curdied: *congealed*   67 dear Valeria; *cf. n.*
69 by . . . time: *when full growth has shown what he is*
71 inform: *inspire*   73 stick: *stand conspicuous*
74 sea-mark: *beacon*   flaw: *squall of wind*
75 eye: *take as guide*

Are suitors to you.

   Cor.   I beseech you, peace:
Or, if you'd ask, remember this before:
The things I have forsworn to grant may never   80
Be held by you denials.   Do not bid me
Dismiss my soldiers, or capitulate
Again with Rome's mechanics: tell me not
Wherein I seem unnatural: desire not   84
To allay my rages and revenges with
Your colder reasons.

   Vol.   O! no more, no more;
You have said you will not grant us anything;
For we have nothing else to ask but that   88
Which you deny already: yet we will ask;
That, if you fail in our request, the blame
May hang upon your hardness.   Therefore, hear us.

   Cor. Aufidius, and you Volsces, mark; for we'll   92
Hear nought from Rome in private.   Your request?

   Vol. Should we be silent and not speak, our raiment
And state of bodies would bewray what life
We have led since thy exile.   Think with thyself   96
How more unfortunate than all living women
Are we come hither: since that thy sight, which should
Make our eyes flow with joy, hearts dance with com-
       forts,   99
Constrains them weep and shake with fear and sorrow;
Making the mother, wife, and child to see
The son, the husband, and the father tearing
His country's bowels out.   And to poor we
Thine enmity's most capital: thou barr'st us   104
Our prayers to the gods, which is a comfort
That all but we enjoy; for how can we,

82 capitulate: *make terms*   90 fail in: *disappoint us in*
95 state of bodies: *physical health*   bewray: *disclose*
103 we: *us*   104 capital: *fatal*

Alas! how can we for our country pray,
Whereto we are bound, together with thy victory,   108
Whereto we are bound?   Alack! or we must lose
The country, our dear nurse, or else thy person,
Our comfort in the country.   We must find
An evident calamity, though we had   112
Our wish, which side should win; for either thou
Must, as a foreign recreant, be led
With manacles through our streets, or else
Triumphantly tread on thy country's ruin,   116
And bear the palm for having bravely shed
Thy wife and children's blood.   For myself, son,
I purpose not to wait on Fortune till
These wars determine: if I cannot persuade thee   120
Rather to show a noble grace to both parts
Than seek the end of one, thou shalt no sooner
March to assault thy country than to tread—
Trust to 't, thou shalt not—on thy mother's womb,   124
That brought thee to this world.
   Vir.   Ay, and mine,
That brought you forth this boy, to keep your name
Living to time.
   Boy.   A' shall not tread on me:
I'll run away till I am bigger, but then I'll fight.   128
   Cor. Not of a woman's tenderness to be,
Requires nor child nor woman's face to see.
I have sat too long.   [*Rising.*]
   Vol.   Nay, go not from us thus.
If it were so, that our request did tend   132
To save the Romans, thereby to destroy
The Volsces whom you serve, you might condemn us,

109 or: *either*   113 which: *in determining which*
114 foreign recreant: *one whose treachery has made him a foreigner*
120 determine: *end*   122 end: *destruction*
129 Not . . . be: *not to yield to womanly weakness*

As poisonous of your honour: no; our suit
Is, that you reconcile them: while the Volsces   136
May say, 'This mercy we have show'd'; the Romans,
'This we receiv'd'; and each in either side
Give the all-hail to thee, and cry, 'Be bless'd
For making up this peace!'   Thou know'st, great
    son,   140
The end of war's uncertain; but this certain,
That, if thou conquer Rome, the benefit
Which thou shalt thereby reap is such a name
Whose repetition will be dogg'd with curses;   144
Whose chronicle thus writ: 'The man was noble,
But with his last attempt he wip'd it out,
Destroy'd his country, and his name remains
To th' ensuing age abhorr'd.'   Speak to me, son!   148
Thou hast affected the fine strains of honour,
To imitate the graces of the gods;
To tear with thunder the wide cheeks o' the air,
And yet to charge thy sulphur with a bolt   152
That should but rive an oak.   Why dost not speak?
Think'st thou it honourable for a nobleman
Still to remember wrongs?   Daughter, speak you:
He cares not for your weeping.   Speak thou, boy: 156
Perhaps thy childishness will move him more
Than can our reasons.   There is no man in the world
More bound to 's mother; yet here he lets me prate
Like one i' the stocks.   Thou hast never in thy life 160
Show'd thy dear mother any courtesy;
When she—poor hen! fond of no second brood—
Has cluck'd thee to the wars, and safely home,

139 all-hail: *formal acclamation*
146 attempt: *undertaking*   it: *his nobility*
149 fine strains: *special refinements*   151 cheeks . . . air; *cf. n.*
152, 153 And yet . . . oak; *cf. n.*   159 prate: *talk without result*
160 one . . . stocks: *a prisoner who has nothing free but his voice*
161 courtesy: *particular favor*

Loaden with honour. Say my request's unjust,   164
And spurn me back; but if it be not so,
Thou art not honest, and the gods will plague thee,
That thou restrain'st from me the duty which
To a mother's part belongs. He turns away: 168
Down, ladies; let us shame him with our knees.
To his surname Coriolanus longs more pride
Than pity to our prayers. Down: an end;
This is the last: so we will home to Rome,   172
And die among our neighbours. Nay, behold 's.
This boy, that cannot tell what he would have,
But kneels and holds up hands for fellowship,
Does reason our petition with more strength   176
Than thou hast to deny 't. Come, let us go:
This fellow had a Volscian to his mother;
His wife is in Corioli, and his child
Like him by chance. Yet give us our dispatch: 180
I am hush'd until our city be a-fire,
And then I'll speak a little.
    Cor.   O, mother, mother!
                Holds her by the hand silent.
What have you done? Behold! the heavens do ope,
The gods look down, and this unnatural scene   184
They laugh at. O my mother! mother! O!
You have won a happy victory to Rome;
But, for your son, believe it, O believe it,
Most dangerously you have with him prevail'd,   188
If not most mortal to him. But let it come.
Aufidius, though I cannot make true wars,
I'll frame convenient peace. Now, good Aufidius,

166 honest: *honorable*   170 longs: *belongs*
175 for fellowship: *to keep us company*
176 Does . . . strength: *has stronger arguments in favor of our peti-tion*   181 hush'd: *silent*
189 most mortal: *with most mortal results*
191 convenient: *a fitting*

Were you in my stead, would you have heard   192
A mother less, or granted less, Aufidius?

Auf. I was mov'd withal.

'*Cor.*   I dare be sworn you were:
And, sir, it is no little thing to make
Mine eyes to sweat compassion. But, good sir,   196
What peace you'll make, advise me: for my part,
I'll not to Rome, I'll back with you: and pray you,
Stand to me in this cause. O mother! wife!

Auf. [*Aside.*] I am glad thou hast set thy mercy and
    thy honour   200
At difference in thee: out of that I'll work
Myself a former fortune.

                    [*The ladies make signs to Coriolanus.*]

Cor.   Ay, by and by;
But we will drink together; and you shall bear
A better witness back than words, which we,   204
On like conditions, would have counterseal'd.
Come, enter with us. Ladies, you deserve
To have a temple built you: all the swords
In Italy, and her confederate arms,   208
Could not have made this peace.   *Exeunt.*

Scene Four

[*Rome.   A Public Place*]

Enter Menenius and Sicinius.

Men. See you yond coign o' the Capitol, yond
corner-stone?

194 withal: *therewith*   196 sweat compassion: *weep with pity*
199 Stand to: *support*
202 a . . . fortune: *a position as great as formerly*
204 A better witness: *i.e. a formal document*
205 *If conditions had been reversed, should have been glad to confirm
    strongly*   208 her . . . arms: *the weapons of Italy's allies*
1 coign: *keystone*

Sic. Why, what of that?

Men. If it be possible for you to displace it 4
with your little finger, there is some hope the
ladies of Rome, especially his mother, may
prevail with him.   But I say, there is no hope
in 't.   Our throats are sentenced and stay upon 8
execution.

Sic. Is 't possible that so short a time can alter
the condition of a man?

Men. There is difference between a grub and 12
a butterfly; yet your butterfly was a grub.   This
Martius is grown from man to dragon: he has
wings; he's more than a creeping thing.

Sic. He loved his mother dearly.   16

Men. So did he me; and he no more remem-
bers his mother now than an eight-year-old
horse.   The tartness of his face sours ripe
grapes: when he walks, he moves like an engine, 20
and the ground shrinks before his treading: he
is able to pierce a corslet with his eye; talks like
a knell, and his 'hum!' is a battery.   He sits in his
state, as a thing made for Alexander.   What 24
he bids be done is finished with his bidding.   He
wants nothing of a god but eternity and a heaven
to throne in.

Sic. Yes, mercy, if you report him truly.   28

Men. I paint him in the character.   Mark what
mercy his mother shall bring from him: there is
no more mercy in him than there is milk in a

---

8 stay upon: *await*   12 differency: *difference*
20 engine: *piece of artillery*   22 corslet: *breastplate*
22, 23 talks . . . battery; *cf. n.*
24 state: *chair of state*   as . . . Alexander: *like a statue of Alex-*
   ander the Great
25 finished . . . bidding: *as good as done when he commands it*
27 throne: *enthrone himself*   29 in . . . character: *as he is*

male tiger; that shall our poor city find: and 32
all this is long of you.

Sic. The gods be good unto us!

Men. No, in such a case the gods will not be
good unto us.　When we banished him, we 36
respected not them; and, he returning to break
our necks, they respect not us.

Enter a Messenger.

Mess. Sir, if you'd save your life, fly to your house:
The plebeians have got your fellow-tribune,　　　40
And hale him up and down; all swearing, if
The Roman ladies bring not comfort home,
They'll give him death by inches.

Enter another Messenger.

Sic.　　　　　　　　　　　　　　What's the news?

Mess. Good news, good news! the ladies have pre-
　　vail'd,　　　　　　　　　　　　　　　　44
The Volscians are dislodg'd, and Martius gone.
A merrier day did never yet greet Rome,
No, not th' expulsion of the Tarquins.

Sic.　　　　　　　　　　　　　　　　Friend,
Art thou certain this is true?　Is 't most certain?　48

Mess. As certain as I know the sun is fire:
Where have you lurk'd that you make doubt of it?
Ne'er through an arch so hurried the blown tide,
As the recomforted through the gates.　Why, hark
　　you!　　　　　　　　　　　　　　　52

Trumpets, hautboys, drums beat, all together.
The trumpets, sackbuts, psalteries, and fifes,

33 long of: *on account of*　　　　　　　37 respected: *heeded*
43 by inches: *by slow torture*
45 are dislodg'd: *have broken camp*　　51 blown: *swollen; cf. n.*
53 sackbuts: *bass wind instruments, trombones*　　psalteries: *stringed*
　　instruments, dulcimers

Tabors, and cymbals, and the shouting Romans,
Make the sun dance.   Hark you!   *A shout within.*
 Men.   This is good news:
I will go meet the ladies.   This Volumnia 56
Is worth of consuls, senators, patricians,
A city full; of tribunes, such as you,
A sea and land full.   You have pray'd well to-day:
This morning for ten thousand of your throats 60
I'd not have given a doit.   Hark, how they joy!
       Sound still with the shouts.
 Sic. First, the gods bless you for your tidings; next,
Accept my thankfulness.
 Mess.   Sir, we have all
Great cause to give great thanks.
 Sic.   They are near the city? 64
 Mess. Almost at point to enter.
 Sic.   We'll meet them,
And help the joy.   *Exeunt.*

*Enter two Senators, with Ladies, passing over the
Stage, with other Lords.*

 Sen. Behold our patroness, the life of Rome!
Call all your tribes together, praise the gods, 68
And make triumphant fires; strew flowers before them:
Unshout the noise that banish'd Martius;
Repeal him with the welcome of his mother;
Cry, 'Welcome, ladies, welcome!'
 All.   Welcome, ladies, 72
Welcome! *A flourish with drums and trumpets.*
            [Exeunt.]

55 Make . . . dance; *cf. n.*
66 S. d. *Cf. n.*   69 fires: *bonfires*
70 Unshout: *cancel and retract by your shouts*

Scene Five

[*Corioli.   A Public Place*]

Enter Tullus Aufidius, with Attendants.

Auf. Go tell the lords o' the city I am here:
Deliver them this paper: having read it,
Bid them repair to the market-place; where I,
Even in theirs and in the commons' ears,   4
Will vouch the truth of it.   Him I accuse
The city ports by this hath enter'd, and
Intends to appear before the people, hoping
To purge himself with words: dispatch.   8
                              [*Exeunt Attendants.*]

Enter three or four Conspirators of Aufidius' faction.

Most welcome !
    1. Con. How is it with our general?
    Auf.   Even so
As with a man by his own alms empoison'd,
And with his charity slain.
    2. Con.   Most noble sir,   12
If you do hold the same intent wherein
You wish'd us parties, we'll deliver you
Of your great danger.
    Auf.   Sir, I cannot tell:
We must proceed as we do find the people.   16
    3. Con. The people will remain uncertain whilst
'Twixt you there's difference; but the fall of either
Makes the survivor heir of all.
    Auf.   I know it;
And my pretext to strike at him admits   20

Scene Five Corioli; *cf. n.*   6 city ports: *gates of the city*
8 purge: *clear*   14 parties: *to take part*
18 difference: *dispute*   20 pretext: *design*

A good construction.   I rais'd him, and I pawn'd
Mine honour for his truth: who being so heighten'd,
He water'd his new plants with dews of flattery,
Seducing so my friends; and, to this end,   24
He bow'd his nature, never known before
But to be rough, unswayable, and free.
   3. Con. Sir, his stoutness
When he did stand for consul, which he lost   28
By lack of stooping,—
   Auf.   That I would have spoke of:
Being banish'd for 't, he came unto my hearth;
Presented to my knife his throat: I took him;
Made him joint-servant with me; gave him way   32
In all his own desires; nay, let him choose
Out of my files, his projects to accomplish,
My best and freshest men; serv'd his designments
In mine own person; holp to reap the fame   36
Which he did end all his; and took some pride
To do myself this wrong: till, at the last,
I seem'd his follower, not partner; and
He wag'd me with his countenance, as if   40
I had been mercenary.
   1. Con.   So he did, my lord:
The army marvell'd at it; and, in the last,
When we had carried Rome, and that we look'd
For no less spoil than glory,—
   Auf.   There was it;   44
For which my sinews shall be stretch'd upon him.

21 good construction: *justification*
23 *By flattery he increased his power in his new environment*
26 free: *independent*   32 way: *freedom of action*
34 files: *troops*
35, 36 serv'd . . . person: *personally assisted him in his designs*
?7 end: *garner, store away*
40 wag'd: *rewarded*   countenance: *patronizing favor*
42 in the last: *finally*
45 my sinews . . . stretch'd: *I shall exert all my force*

At a few drops of women's rheum, which are
As cheap as lies, he sold the blood and labour
Of our great action: therefore shall he die,   48
And I'll renew me in his fall.   But, hark!

> *Drums and trumpets sound, with great shouts*
> *of the people.*

1. Con. Your native town you enter'd like a post,
And had no welcomes home; but he returns,
Splitting the air with noise.

2. Con.   And patient fools,   52
Whose children he hath slain, their base throats tear
With giving him glory.

3. Con.   Therefore, at your vantage,
Ere he express himself, or move the people
With what he would say, let him feel your sword,   56
Which we will second.   When he lies along,
After your way his tale pronounc'd shall bury
His reasons with his body.

Auf.   Say no more:
Here come the lords.   60

> *Enter the Lords of the City.*

All Lords. You are most welcome home.

Auf.   I have not deserv'd it.
But, worthy lords, have you with heed perus'd
What I have written to you?

All.   We have.

1. Lord.   And grieve to hear 't.
What faults he made before the last, I think,   64
Might have found easy fines; but there to end

46 rheum: *tears, liquid secretion*   50 post: *messenger*
54 at . . . vantage: *as soon as favorable opportunity arises*
57 along: *prostrate*
58 After . . . pronounc'd: *your statement of his case*
59 His reasons: *what he might urge in his behalf*
65 fines: *penalties*

Where he was to begin, and give away
The benefit of our levies, answering us
With our own charge, making a treaty where   68
There was a yielding, this admits no excuse.

Auf. He approaches: you shall hear him.

*Enter Coriolanus, marching with drums and colours;
the Commoners being with him.*

Cor. Hail, lords! I am return'd your soldier;
No more infected with my country's love   72
Than when I parted hence, but still subsisting
Under your great command.   You are to know,
That prosperously I have attempted and
With bloody passage led your wars even to   76
The gates of Rome.   Our spoils we have brought home
Do more than counterpoise a full third part
The charges of the action.   We have made peace
With no less honour to the Antiates   80
Than shame to the Romans; and we here deliver,
Subscrib'd by the consuls and patricians,
Together with the seal o' the senate, what
We have compounded on.

Auf.   Read it not, noble lords;   84
But tell the traitor, in the highest degree
He hath abus'd your powers.

Cor. Traitor! How now?

Auf.   Ay, traitor, Martius.

Cor.   Martius!

Auf. Ay, Martius, Caius Martius.   Dost thou
    think   88

67 benefit . . . levies: *profits of war*   answering: *repaying; cf. n.*
68 treaty: *compromise*
69 yielding: *complete defeat of the enemy*
72 infected: *affected, contaminated*
75 prosperously . . . attempted: *my attempts have prospered*
77 we have: *which we have*   84 compounded: *agreed*

I'll grace thee with that robbery, thy stol'n name,
Coriolanus in Corioli?
You lords and heads o' the state, perfidiously
He has betray'd your business, and given up,   92
For certain drops of salt, your city Rome,
I say 'your city,' to his wife and mother;
Breaking his oath and resolution like
A twist of rotten silk, never admitting   96
Counsel o' the war, but at his nurse's tears
He whin'd and roar'd away your victory,
That pages blush'd at him, and men of heart
Look'd wondering each at others.

> *Cor.*   Hear'st thou, Mars? 100
> *Auf.* Name not the god, thou boy of tears.
> *Cor.*   Ha!
> *Auf.* No more.
> *Cor.* Measureless liar, thou hast made my heart
Too great for what contains it.   Boy! O slave!   104
Pardon me, lords, 'tis the first time that ever
I was forc'd to scold.   Your judgments, my grave
          lords,
Must give this cur the lie: and his own notion—
Who wears my stripes impress'd upon him, that   108
Must bear my beating to his grave—shall join
To thrust the lie unto him.

> *1. Lord.* Peace, both, and hear me speak.

> *Cor.* Cut me to pieces, Volsces; men and lads,   112
Stain all your edges on me.   Boy!   False hound!
If you have writ your annals true, 'tis there,
That, like an eagle in a dove-cote, I

96 twist: *skein*
96, 97 never . . . war: *permitting no council of war*
99 That pages: *so that young boys*   men of heart: *valiant men*
104 Too . . . it: *swollen with indignation till my breast cannot con-
      tain it*   107 notion: *intelligence*
108 that: *who*

Flutter'd your Volscians in Corioli: 116
Alone I did it. Boy!

Auf.   Why, noble lords,
Will you be put in mind of his blind fortune,
Which was your shame, by this unholy braggart,
'Fore your own eyes and ears?

All Consp.   Let him die for 't. 120

All People. Tear him to pieces.—Do it
presently.—He killed my son.—My daughter.
—He killed my cousin Marcus.—He killed my
father.   124

2. Lord. Peace, ho! no outrage: peace!
The man is noble and his fame folds in
This orb o' the earth. His last offences to us
Shall have judicious hearing. Stand, Aufidius,   128
And trouble not the peace.

Cor.   O that I had him,
With six Aufidiuses, or more, his tribe,
To use my lawful sword!

Auf.   Insolent villain!

All. Consp. Kill, kill, kill, kill, kill him!

> *Draw all the Conspirators, and kill Martius,*
> *who falls. Aufidius stands on him.*

Lords.   Hold, hold, hold, hold! 132

Auf. My noble masters, hear me speak.

1. Lord.   O Tullus!

2. Lord. Thou hast done a deed whereat valour will
    weep.

3. Lord. Tread not upon him, masters; all be quiet.
Put up your swords.   136

Auf. My lords, when you shall know,—as in this
    rage,

116 Flutter'd: *put to flight*
128 judicious: *judicial, legal*   Stand: *stay, hold*

Provok'd by him, you cannot,—the great danger
Which this man's life did owe you, you'll rejoice
That he is thus cut off.   Please it your honours   140
To call me to your senate, I'll deliver
Myself your loyal servant, or endure
Your heaviest censure.

    1. Lord.   Bear from hence his body;
And mourn you for him!   Let him be regarded   144
As the most noble corse that ever herald
Did follow to his urn.

    2. Lord.   His own impatience
Takes from Aufidius a great part of blame.
Let's make the best of it.

    Auf.   My rage is gone,   148
And I am struck with sorrow.   Take him up:
Help, three o' the chiefest soldiers; I'll be one.
Beat thou the drum, that it speak mournfully;
Trail your steel pikes.   Though in this city he   152
Hath widow'd and unchilded many a one,
Which to this hour bewail the injury,
Yet he shall have a noble memory.

Assist.   *Exeunt, bearing the body of Martius.*
                                  A dead march sounded.

139 did owe you: *promised to bring upon you, rendered you liable to*
141 deliver: *demonstrate*
152 Trail: *drag on the ground in sign of mourning*
153 unchilded: *slain the children of*

FINIS.

NOTES

I. i. 36. *2. Cit.* The Folio gives this line to *'All.'*
The later speeches of the Second Citizen, beginning
with that at line 59, are transferred by Capell and
other editors to the First Citizen on the ground that
the Second Citizen has shown himself friendly to
Martius. He is, however, a convinced supporter of
the people's rights.

I. i. 97. *To scale't a little more.* 'Scale' is probably used in the sense of put it on the scales, weigh
its meaning. Compare 'Scaling' in II. iii. 257. Theobald has been followed by most editors in emending
to 'stale.'

I. i. 114. *Which ne'er came from the lungs.* A
quiet reflective smile with nothing boisterous about it.

I. i. 116. *taintingly.* Modern editors agree in
emending to 'tauntingly,' but the belly is not taunting.
To taint means to make a successful hit in tilting.

I. i. 122. *The counsellor heart.* The heart was
supposed to be the seat of reason. Compare line 142.

I. i. 165. *Thou rascal, that art worst in blood to
run.* You who are in the worst physical condition for
running (or other activity). A rascal was a lean,
inferior deer, whereas stags were said to be 'in blood'
when in good condition. Compare IV. v. 226.

I. i. 171, 172. *That, rubbing the poor itch of your
opinion, Make yourselves scabs.* There is a pun on
'scabs': (a) scabby sores, (b) good-for-nothing citizens.

I. i. 178, 179. *you are no surer, no, Than is the coal
of fire upon the ice.* The Thames River was frozen
over in the winter of 1608 (a rare phenomenon), and
fires were built upon the ice. This figure has therefore been used in dating the play.

I. i. 180-182. *Your virtue is, To make him worthy whose offence subdues him, And curse that justice did it.* 'Your kindness shows itself only in espousing the cause of the punished delinquent and in cursing the justice which made him suffer.

I. i. 266, 267. *disdains the shadow Which he treads on at noon.* 'The sun being vertical at noon, a man treads on his own shadow then.' (Arden ed.)

I. ii. 27. *Corioli.* The name had been gallicized by Amyot into 'Corioles.' It is retained in this form by North and usually in the Shakespeare Folio. (In the stage direction at the opening of this scene the Folio spells it 'Coriolus.')

I. iii. 16. *his brows bound with oak.* Crowned with a wreath of oak leaves. Plutarch (North) records that in an early battle the young Martius saved the life of a Roman soldier. 'Hereupon, after the battle was won, the Dictator did not forget so noble an act, and therefore first of all he crowned Martius with a garland of oaken boughs. For whosoever saveth the life of a Roman, it is a manner among them to honour him with such a garland.'

I. iv. 14. *No, nor a man that fears you less than he.* Logical syntax requires 'more' instead of 'less.' Shakespeare frequently makes slips of this sort.

I. iv. 34. *Against the wind a mile.* Let the infection be so great as to carry a mile against the wind.

I. iv. 42. *As they us to our trenches follows.* As they are now following us to our trenches. Instances of the old northern English plural in -s abound in Shakespeare.

I. iv. 56, 57. *Thou wast a soldier Even to Cato's wish.* This passage, to line 61, is a close adaptation of North's words: 'For he was even such another as Cato would have a soldier and a captain to be, not only terrible and fierce to lay about him, but to make the enemy afeared with the sound of his voice and grimness of his countenance.' Shakespeare's transfer of the speech to the mouth of a contemporary of Coriolanus produces a striking anachronism, since Martius lived some three hundred years before Cato the Censor (234-149 B.C.).

I. v. 6, 7. *doublets that hangmen would Bury with those that wore them.* An allusion to the Elizabethan custom which made the garments of executed prisoners a perquisite of the hangman. Doublets (jackets) which a hangman would refuse to take would not be worth the plunderers' while to steal.

I. vi. 6. *The Roman gods.* O you, the gods of Rome! It is not necessary to alter 'The' to 'Ye,' as is commonly done. The reading of the text is an authorized vocative construction in Elizabethan English.

I. vi. 76. [*Soldiers.*] *O, me alone! Make you a sword of me!* The Folio prints the line without indication of speaker, but it is difficult to explain it as part of Martius' speech.

I. viii. 12, 13. *Wert thou the Hector That was the whip of your bragg'd progeny.* 'Progeny' means race or stock, and 'whip' the scourge with which punishment is inflicted: 'If you were Hector, the most formidable warrior of your boasted race.' Allusion is made, of course, to the asserted descent of the Romans from the Trojans.

I. ix. 31. *tent themselves with death.* Make death the means of cleansing themselves from festering ingratitude.

I. ix. 46. *Let him be made an overture for the wars.* Tyrwhitt and most modern editors alter 'an overture' to 'a coverture,' without much assisting the interpretation of the line. The Folio text appears to mean, 'Let an offer of warlike employment be made to him (the parasite).' When soldiers adopt the effeminate ways of courtiers, let us recruit our armies among the latter class.

II. i. 42-44. *O that you could turn your eyes towards the napes of your necks, and make but an interior survey of your good selves.* 'The original fable of Æsop, reproduced by Phædrus, IV. 10, was that Jupiter has furnished every man with two wallets, one hanging down on his breast and containing his neighbour's faults, which are always before his eyes, and the other hanging down his back out of sight, and filled with his own faults.' (Arden ed.) A variation of the fable is found in *Troilus and Cressida*, III. iii. 145 f., where Ulysses says:

> 'Time hath, my lord, a wallet at his back,
> Wherein he puts alms for oblivion.'

II. i. 53, 54. *a cup of hot wine with not a drop of allaying Tiber in 't.* This passage apparently suggested Lovelace's famous lines (*To Althœa from Prison*):

> 'When flowing cups run swiftly round
> With no allaying Thames.'

II. i. 57-59. *one that converses more with the buttock of the night than with the forehead of the morning.* Better acquainted with the last hour of the night than the first hour of the morning.

II. i. 63-66. *I cannot say your worships have delivered the matter well when I find the ass in compound with the major part of your syllables.* I cannot compliment you on your statement of the case against Martius when the larger part of what you say cries out 'ass!' against you—convicts you of asininity.

II. i. 70. *the map of my microcosm.* My face. Menenius' microcosm or little world was himself and his face the map or chart which summarized its characteristics.

II. i. 72. *bisson conspectuities.* No other example of 'conspectuities' appears to be known. It is doubtless an intentionally pretentious coinage from Latin *conspectus,* sight. The Folio spelling of 'bisson' is 'beesome.'

II. i. 91-93. *Come, come, you are well understood to be a perfecter giber for the table than a necessary bencher in the Capitol.* It is well known that you are better fitted to be a jesting table-companion than a serviceable senator.

II. i. 168. *the repulse of Tarquin.* Plutarch says (North): 'The first time he went to the wars, being but a stripling, was when Tarquin surnamed the proud (that had been king of Rome, and was driven out for his pride . . .) did come to Rome with all the aid of the Latins, and many other people of Italy . . . who with a great and mighty army had undertaken to put him into his kingdom again.' The battle referred to, the last of four attempts to restore King Tarquin, occurred in 499 B.C. Shakespeare makes Cominius tell the story of Martius' exploits on this occasion. See II. ii. 92 ff.

II. i. 170. *there's nine that I know.* Shakespeare often seems resentful of mathematical precision. One would expect a total of ten here. Some commentators improbably suggest that Menenius makes a fresh count to himself, ending with 'One i' the neck,' etc.

II. i. 194. *My gracious silence.* Mr. Case (Arden ed.) suggests that Shakespeare may have derived this pretty nickname of Virgilia from North's translation of Plutarch's Life of Numa, where it is stated that the hero 'taught the Romans to reverence one of [the Muses] above all the rest, who was called Tacita, as ye would say *Lady Silence.*'

II. i. 200. *I know not where to turn.* I retain, doubtfully, the arrangement of modern editors. The Folio gives line 199 to Cominius, not Coriolanus, which would better explain Volumnia's words. If 199 really belongs to Coriolanus, it is possible that 'I know

. . . turn' should also be assigned to him and Volumnia's speech begin 'O! welcome home,' which commences a new line in the Folio.

II. i. 204. *A curse begin at very root on's heart.* May a curse strike home at once to the most vital part! The common emendation, 'begnaw' for 'begin,' is unnecessary.

II. i. 223 S. d. *Enter Brutus and Sicinius.* That is, they now come forward.

II. i. 243, 244. *He cannot temperately transport his honours From where he should begin and end.* He cannot, as a self-restrained man could, derive honor from both the beginning and the completion of his performances. He cannot go an equable pace and conclude with the same honors with which he begins.

II. i. 272-274. *This, as you say, suggested At some time when his soaring insolence Shall teach the people.* If we time our incitement to some occasion when his insolence shall confirm it in the people's mind. Instead of 'teach' Hanmer suggested 'touch' and Theobald 'reach.' The former is a very plausible correction, but not inevitable.

II. ii. 93, 94. *he fought Beyond the mark of others.* In fighting he surpassed all that others could do. Compare note on II. i. 168.

II. ii. 106. *He lurch'd all swords of the garland.* Evidence for the date of *Coriolanus* has been found in the fact that Ben Jonson appears to have imitated this passage in the last speech of his *Silent Woman* (1609 or 1610), where Truewit says: 'Well, Dauphine, you have lurch'd your friends of the better half of the garland.'

II. iii. 65 S. d. *Enter two of the Citizens.* The Folio indicates the number as 'three' and assigns the speeches at lines 68, 73, 76, and 87 to '*3. Cit.*'; but Coriolanus alludes to them as 'a brace' (l. 66) and 'two worthy voices' (l. 85).

II. iii. 122. *wolfish toge.* Wolf's toga, or garment. Why should I stand here like a wolf in sheep's clothing? The first Folio has 'Wooluish tongue,' and the later Folios 'Woolvish gowne.' One of the best of many emendations is 'woolless toge.'

II. iii. 251. *And Censorinus, that was so surnam'd.* This line is omitted by the Folio, evidently by inadvertence, since 252 makes no sense immediately after 250. The present line is Delius' emendation, based upon the words of North in the opening passage of the Life of Coriolanus, which Brutus' speech paraphrases closely. North translates: 'Of the same house were Publius and Quintus, who brought Rome their best water they had by conducts. *Censorinus* also came of that family, *that was so surnamed* because the people had chosen him Censor twice.' It may be that the Folio printer was confused by two consecutive lines beginning with 'And,' and accidentally omitted the first.

III. i. 128. *motive.* Johnson's emendation for 'Natiue' of the Folio.

III. i. 130, 131. *How shall this bosom multiplied digest The senate's courtesy?* This is the Folio reading, which editors have unjustifiably emended. 'This bosom multiplied' means this composite bosom, the bosom of this conglomerate rabble. Compare *King Lear* V. iii. 47-50:

'the old and miserable king . . .
Whose age has charms in it, whose title more,
To pluck the common bosom on his side.'

Shakespeare frequently uses 'bosom' for the seat of digestion, or rather the part of the body in which indigestion makes itself felt; thus in *2 Henry IV* I. iii. 91-98:

'O thou fond many ! . . .
So, so, thou common dog, didst thou disgorge
Thy glutton bosom of the royal Richard.'

III. i. 212. *the rock Tarpeian.* A part of the Capitoline hill, down which condemned criminals were cast to death.

III. i. 304-306. *The service of the foot, Being once gangren'd, is not then respected For what before it was.* Menenius is elaborating his statement in lines 294, 295, that the 'disease' in Coriolanus, which causes the plebeians to dislike him, is curable. Brutus, however, interrupts him.

III. ii. 21. *The thwartings of.* Theobald's emendation. The Folio reads 'The things of,' which does not make sense. In line 32, below, Theobald has again been followed in substituting 'herd' for the 'heart' of the Folio.

III. ii. 55, 56. *such words that are but rooted in Your tongue.* The Folio spells 'roated,' which can be interpreted as 'roted,' learned by rote, parrot-like; but one would then expect the following preposition to be 'on' rather than 'in.'

III. ii. 71, 72. *Not what is dangerous present, but the loss Of what is past.* Not only apply a healing salve to the present danger, but also save what you have already lost. 'Salve' in line 70 has a different sense with each of the object clauses.

III. ii. 74, 75. *And thus far having stretch'd it,— here be with them,—Thy knee bussing the stones.* Stretching your conciliatory gestures to the point (do this to please their mood) of letting your knee caress the paving stones.

III. iii. 11. *Have you collected them by tribes?* This, like the counting of votes 'by the poll' (line 10), was a device to give weight to the plebeian vote. North says: 'And first of all the Tribunes would in any case (whatsoever became of it) that the people would proceed to give their voices by Tribes, and not by hundreds: for by this means the multitude of the poor needy people (and all such rabble as had nothing to lose, and had less regard of honesty before their eyes) came to be of greater force (because their voices were numbered by the poll) than the noble honest citizens, whose persons and purse did dutifully serve the commonwealth in their wars.' The division of Roman citizens into tribes (originally three, finally thirty-five) was democratic, while the division into 193 hundreds (centuriæ) was based upon property qualifications.

III. iii. 54. *accents*. Theobald's universally accepted emendation for the Folio's 'Actions.'

III. iii. 97. *doth*. An old (southern) plural. The second Folio normalized it to 'doe.'

III. iii. 133 S. d. *with others*. The Folio gives this in the remarkably corrupted form, 'with Cumalijs' (i.e. *cum aliis*). The 'others' are the rest of the patricians. The next word, 'They,' refers to the plebeians.

IV. i. 7-9. *fortune's blows, When most struck home,—being gentle, wounded, craves A noble cunning*. 'When Fortune strikes her hardest blows, to be wounded, and yet continue calm, requires a generous policy.' (Johnson.) The construction of the sentence is suddenly changed in the middle (anacoluthon): 'fortune's blows,' originally intended as subject, is left hanging as an 'absolute nominative,' and a new subject, 'being gentle,' is introduced.

IV. ii. 16. *mankind*. Sicinius uses the word in the invidious sense in which it was applied to women: virago-like. Volumnia in the next line takes it as meaning 'human' in contrast with the 'foxship' of Sicinius.

IV. ii. 52. *Leave this faint puling.* Volumnia addresses Virgilia, who is weeping silently.

IV. iv. 13. *Whose double bosoms seems to wear one heart.* The verbal plural in -s (cf. note on I. iv. 42), perhaps here used with some idea of the apparent unity of the 'double bosoms.'

IV. iv. 20. *To take the one the other.* Construe with 'plots' in line 19: plots by which the one hopes to get the better of the other.

IV. iv. 23. *My birth-place hate I.* For 'hate' the Folio misprints 'haue.'

IV. v. 137. *o'er-bear.* The Folio has 'o're-beate,' which a few editors defend.

IV. v. 153 S. d. *Enter two of the Servingmen.* That is, the Servingmen, who have been auditors, now advance. Compare II. i. 223 S. d.

IV. v. 172. *but a greater soldier than he you wot on.* The Folio reading is 'but a greater soldier than he, you wot one,' i.e., you know one greater soldier (Aufidius) than he. This can be justified, but Dyce's emendation, as given in the text, seems preferable. In any case the servants are speaking cautiously, drawing each other out.

IV. v. 201. *boiled.* Culinary editors, led by Pope, alter to 'broiled,' since that is the proper treatment of a 'carbonado' steak.

IV. vi. 2. *tame i' the present peace.* Theobald added the preposition. The Folio reads: 'His remedies are tame, the present peace.'

IV. vi. 44. *Thrusts forth his horns again.* The allusion is to the action of a snail. See next line.

IV. vi. 59. *some news is coming.* Rowe has been usually followed in altering 'coming' to 'come,' but Shakespeare is fond of the conception of news as gradually unfolded by 'sequent messengers,' whose reports vary and cause uncertainty or suspense. Compare *Othello* I. ii. 41 and the opening of the following scene in that play; also *2 Henry IV* I. i.

IV. vi. 68, 69. *And vows revenge as spacious as between The young'st and oldest thing.* Vows to include every living thing in his revenge.

IV. vi. 86. *Your temples burned in their cement.* Subjected to such conflagration that even the mortar will be consumed. As always in Shakespeare, 'cement' is accented on the first syllable.

IV. vi. 113, 114. *they charg'd him even As those should do that had deserv'd his hate.* By asking him to spare Rome his friends would be making common cause with his foes.

IV. vi. 119. *you have crafted fair.* A pun on 'crafted' is involved: (a) advanced the crafts' interests, (b) shown your craft.

IV. vi. 127-129. *desperation Is all the policy, strength, and defence, That Rome can make against them.* All that Rome can do against them in the way of either negotiation, offence, or defence is a desperate hope.

IV. vii. 24-26. *yet he hath left undone That which shall break his neck or hazard mine, Whene'er we come to our account.* The allusion appears to be to Plutarch's statement that, after Coriolanus had led his army to within forty furlongs of Rome and made great demands on behalf of the Volsci, he omitted to press his advantage and allowed the Romans a respite of thirty days in which to make their answer. 'This,' says North, 'was the first matter wherewith the Volsces (that most envied Martius' glory and authority) did charge Martius with. Among those, Tullus was chief.'

IV. vii. 34, 35. *As is the osprey to the fish, who takes it By sovereignty of nature.* The osprey, or fishhawk, was supposed to have a natural power of fascinating fishes. Editors quote several contemporary statements of the belief; e.g., Peele's *Battle of Alcazar* II. iii.:

> 'I will provide thee with a princely osprey,
> That, as she flieth over fish in pools,
> The fish shall turn their glittering bellies up.'

IV. vii. 42, 43. *not moving From the casque to the cushion.* His nature or disposition not adapting itself to suit the proprieties of conduct in time of war and time of peace respectively. The casque is the symbol of the warrior, the cushion of the senator. Compare III. i. 100 and stage direction at opening of II. ii.

IV. vii. 48, 49. *but he has a merit To choke it in the utterance.* His merit is so great that condemnation of his fault should be silenced ere fully uttered.

IV. vii. 51-53. *And power, unto itself most commendable, Hath not a tomb so evident as a chair To extol what it hath done.* Power, though (when considered absolutely) most worthily attained, is never so near its grave as when the successful man, seated in the chair of authority, seeks to justify the means by which he has risen.

IV. vii. 55. *Rights by rights falter.* One conception of justice hampers another. For 'falter' (Dyce's emendation) the Folio reads 'fouler.' Johnson proposed 'founder.'

V. i. 16. *rack'd.* The word is spelled 'wrack'd' in the Folio; and there is probably a play on the sense of 'rack'd' as explained in the footnote and 'wrack'd,' brought all to wrack and ruin.

V. i. 68-70. *what he would do He sent in writing after me, what he would not, Bound with an oath to yield to his conditions.* He sent a written statement of what he would and would not do, requiring an oath of unconditional acceptance of these conditions.

V. ii. 10. *it is lots to blanks.* It is more likely than not. Lots were the drawings in a lottery, blanks those that carried no prize. The Arden editors have a learned note upon this phrase, the meaning of which is not so simple as it appears.

V. ii. 17. *I have ever verified my friends.* The Folio reading, 'verified,' gives a reasonable sense. Many emendations have, however, been proposed and adopted; e.g., magnified, amplified, glorified.

V. ii. 90, 91. *my remission lies In Volscian breasts.* In exercising clemency I am no free agent, but must be governed by the feelings of the Volsci.

V. ii. 91-93. *That we have been familiar, Ingrate forgetfulness shall poison, rather Than pity note how much.* I shall rather be ungrateful in forgetting our old familiarity than by dwelling upon it allow my pity to be aroused.

V. ii. 110, 111. *He that hath a will to die by himself fears it not from another.* One who, like Menenius, would be willing to slay himself is beyond caring for the death threats of the Watch. Compare line 59, above.

V. iii. 39, 40. *The sorrow that delivers us thus chang'd Makes you think so.* Virgilia purposely misconstrues her husband's words. The great alteration, she says, which sorrow has caused in our appearance makes you think you can't believe your eyes.

V. iii. 51, 52. *Of thy deep duty more impression show Than that of common sons.* Wishing to emphasize his dutiful respect, Coriolanus bids his knee, not simply touch the ground, but sink into it and leave a deep imprint.

V. iii. 67. *dear Valeria.* In Plutarch it is she who suggests to Volumnia and Virgilia the visit to Coriolanus' camp. North speaks of her thus: 'Valeria, Publicola's own sister; the self same Publicola, who did such notable service to the Romans, both in peace and wars, and was dead also certain years before, as we have declared in his life. His sister Valeria was greatly honoured and reverenced among all the Romans; and did so modestly and wisely behave herself, that she did not shame nor dishonour the house she came of.'

V. iii. 151. *To tear with thunder the wide cheeks o' the air.* The allusion is doubtless to the common indication of the winds (north, south, etc.) in old maps as issuing from cherubs' swollen cheeks. In *Richard II,* III. iii. 55-57, Shakespeare speaks of

'the elements
Of fire and water, when their thundering shock
At meeting tears the cloudy cheeks of heaven.'

V. iii. 152, 153. *And yet to charge thy sulphur with a bolt That should but rive an oak.* And yet, with all your terrible show, to commit no inhumanity.

V. iv. 22, 23. *talks like a knell, and his 'hum! is a battery.* His conversation bodes death, and his exclamation of impatience is like the sound of cannon.

V. iv. 51. *Ne'er through an arch so hurried the blown tide.* The allusion is to the rush of the incoming tide through the old London bridge, which consisted of twenty arches. The same figure is found in *Lucrece,* ll. 1667-1671:

'As through an arch the violent roaring tide
Outruns the eye that doth behold his haste,
Yet in the eddy boundeth in his pride
Back to the strait that forc'd him on so fast;
In rage sent out, recall'd in rage, being past.'

V. iv. 55. *Make the sun dance.* An old popular belief was that the sun danced for joy on Easter morning. It is alluded to by many writers of Shakespeare's time.

V. iv. 66 S. d. Some editors make a new scene of the next six lines.

V. v. S. d. *Corioli.* The text of this scene is inconsistent in locating it, first at Antium, the Volscian capital, and later at Corioli. Professor Gordon's explanation is highly satisfactory: 'Editors are divided whether to place this scene in Antium or Corioli. We should expect it to be Antium. Plutarch makes it Antium. But in line 90 it is explicitly said to be Corioli. On the other hand, ll. 50, 73, 80, all point to Antium. We hear in l. 50 that it was Aufidius's native town, which seems to have been Antium (I. vi. 59); in l. 73 that Coriolanus has come back to the place he started from, which was Antium; in l. 80 that peace had been made with honour to "the Antiates." The solution seems to me to be this. Shakespeare meant the scene to be Antium, and wrote with Antium in his mind until he came to Aufidius's speech in l. 88. There he was carried away by the magnificent opportunity of placing "Coriolanus in Corioli" (l. 90), and for the rest of the scene thought rather of Corioli than of Antium.'

V. v. 67, 68. *answering us With our own charge.* Paying us back only the amount of our expenditure, bringing in no profit. Compare lines 77-79, where Coriolanus estimates that the gains from the expedition amount to one-third more than the costs. The point is that no large indemnity had been secured from the Romans.

APPENDIX A

Sources of the Play

The chief and almost sole source of *Coriolanus,* as of Shakespeare's other Roman plays, is North's translation of Plutarch's *Lives,* which was first printed in 1579 and reached its third edition in 1603. About 550 lines of North's prose are woven into the text of *Coriolanus,* and the verbal adherence of the poet to the translator is even closer than it is in the earlier Plutarchan plays of *Julius Cæsar* and *Antony and Cleopatra.* The two principal characters, Coriolanus and Volumnia, owe most to Plutarch, though Shakespeare has given to each of them distinguishing traits hardly implied by his original. Virgilia, Menenius, and the Tribunes, on the other hand, are developed out of very slight suggestions. North only once mentions Virgilia's name and affords us no clue to her character. He says nothing of Menenius' friendship for Coriolanus, and names him only in the following account of his famous fable:

When the Plebeians were threatening to withdraw from Rome, North says: 'The Senate, being afeared of their departure, did send unto them certain of the pleasantest old men and the most acceptable to the people among them. Of those Menenius Agrippa was he who was sent for chief man of the message from the Senate. He, after many good persuasions and gentle requests made to the people on the behalf of the Senate, knit up his oration in the end with a notable tale, in this manner. That on a time all the members of man's body did rebel against the belly, complaining of it, that it only remained in the midst of the body, without doing anything, neither did bear any labour to the maintenance of the rest: whereas all other parts and members did labour painfully, and were very careful to satisfy the appetites and desires of the body. And so the belly, all this notwithstanding, laughed at their folly, and said: "It is true, I first receive all meats that nourish man's body: but afterwards I send it again to the nourishment of other parts of the same." "Even so" (quoth he) "O you, my masters, and citizens of Rome: the reason is a like between the Senate and you. For matters being well digested, and their counsels thoroughly examined, touching the benefit of the commonwealth, the Senators are cause of the common commodity that cometh unto every one of you." These persuasions pacified the people.'

The most famous declamatory passages in *Coriolanus* are precisely those in which Shakespeare has most closely reproduced the prose of North. They are Coriolanus' indictment of the mob (III. i. 63-138), his speech to Aufidius in the latter's house at Antium (IV. v. 71-107), and Volumnia's successful appeal for Rome (V. iii. 94 ff.). These are the emotional crises of the play. They are singular examples of the tact with which at this period of his career Shakespeare could transfer a fine and living picture from narrative to drama and from prose to poetry with the maximum of fidelity and an irreducible minimum of remoulding. North thus reports the speeches of Coriolanus and Aufidius:

'Tullus rose presently from the board, and, coming towards him, asked him what he was, and wherefore he came. Then Martius unmuffled himself, and after he had paused a while, making no answer, he said unto him. "If thou knowest me not yet, Tullus, and, seeing me, dost not perhaps believe me to be the man I am in deed, I must of necessity bewray my self to be that I am. I am Caius Martius, who hath done to thy self particularly, and to all the Volsces generally, great

hurt and mischief, which I cannot deny for my surname of Coriolanus that I bear. For I never had
other benefit nor recompense of all the true and painful
service I have done, and the extreme dangers I have
been in, but this only surname: a good memory and
witness of the malice and displeasure thou shouldst
bear me. Indeed the name only remaineth with me:
for the rest envy and cruelty of the people of Rome
have taken from me, by the sufferance of the dastardly
nobility and magistrates, who have forsaken me, and
let me be banished by the people. This extremity hath
now driven me to come as a poor suitor to take thy
chimney hearth, not of any hope I have to save my life
thereby. For if I had feared death, I would not have
come hither to have put my life in hazard: but pricked
forward with spite and desire I have to be revenged
of them that thus have banished me, whom now I begin
to be avenged on, putting my person between my
enemies. Wherefore, if thou hast any heart to be
wreaked of the injuries thy enemies have done thee,
speed thee now, and let my misery serve thy turn, and
so use it, as my service may be a benefit to the Volsces:
promising thee, that I will fight with better good-will
for all you, than ever I did when I was against you,
knowing that they fight more valiantly, who know the
force of their enemy, than such as have never proved
it. And if it be so that thou dare not, and that thou
art weary to prove fortune any more: then am I also
weary to live any longer. And it were no wisdom in
thee to save the life of him, who hath been heretofore
thy mortal enemy, and whose service now can nothing
help nor pleasure thee." Tullus, hearing what he said,
was a marvellous glad man, and, taking him by the
hand, he said unto him: "Stand up, O Martius, and be
of good cheer, for in proffering thyself unto us thou
dost us great honour: and by this means thou mayest
hope also of greater things at all the Volsces' hands."

So he feasted him for that time, and entertained him in the honourablest manner he could, talking with him in no other matters at that present: but within few days after, they fell to consultation together in what sort 'they should begin their wars.'

Comparison of this passage with its Shakespearean counterpart (IV. v. 55-153) shows that while the speech of Coriolanus is virtually all Plutarch, the speeches of Aufidius are almost wholly original with Shakespeare. They offer an instructive contrast in style and an admirable illustration of the manner in which Shakespeare could make dramatic adaptation go hand in hand with dramatic originality.

In the handling of incident Shakespeare treats Plutarch with the same appreciative discrimination as in the writing of dialogue. Seven scenes of the play are independent of North, and Plutarchan incidents are not infrequently altered to the advantage of dramatic economy, as when Shakespeare makes Coriolanus' yearlong squabbles with the Plebcians all focus upon the election to the Consulship. But when the Plutarchan story is good drama as it stands, the poet hardly tampers with it at all.

For the fable of Menenius, as told in the play (I. i. 94-160) it has been pointed out that Shakespeare appears to have made use of a version more detailed than that which Plutarch gives. This is found in William Camden's *Remaines of a Greater Worke, Concerning Britain,* published in 1605. It will be seen on comparison with North's narrative, quoted on page 158, that the following account, as given by Camden, has a number of verbal similarities with Shakespeare's lines which are absent from North and can hardly have been accidental:—'All the members of the body conspired against the stomacke, as against the swallowing gulfe of all their labors; for whereas the eies beheld, the eares heard, the handes labored, the feete traveled,

the tongue spake, and all partes performed their functions, onely the stomacke lay ydle and consumed all.
Hereuppon they ioyntly agreed al to forbeare their
labors, and to pine away their lasie and publike enemy.
One day passed over, the second followed very tedious,
but the third day was so grievous to them all, that they
called a common Counsel; The eyes waxed dimme, the
feete could not support the body, the armes waxed
lasie, the tongue faltered, and could not lay open the
matter; Therefore they all with one accord desired
the advise of the Heart. There Reason layd open before
them, that hee against whome they had proclaimed
warres, was the cause of all this their misery: For he
as their common steward, when his allowances were
withdrawne, of necessitie withdrew theirs fro them,
as not receiving that he might allow. Therefore it
were a farre better course to supply him, than that
the limbs should faint with hunger. So by the per-
swasion of Reason, the stomacke was served, the limbes
comforted, and peace re-established. Even so it fareth
with the bodies of Common-weales. . . .

APPENDIX B

THE HISTORY OF THE PLAY

Coriolanus is the latest in date of Shakespeare's tragedies. The evidence of style and several unusually persuasive internal allusions[1] point to its composition in 1608 or 1609, immediately after *Antony and Cleopatra*. Of the stage history of the play before the Restoration we have no knowledge whatever.[2] Indeed the earliest positive allusion to it is found in the licensing notice of previously uncopyrighted Shakespearean plays, entered on the book of the Stationers' Company by the publishers of the Shakespeare Folio, November 8, 1623. Here *Coriolanus* is named first among the eight tragedies 'not formerly entred to other men.' In the Folio of 1623, and the three following Folio editions of Shakespeare, *Coriolanus* is accordingly printed between *Troilus and Cressida* and *Titus Andronicus*. These, with the exception of Tate's alteration, are the only texts of the play published during the seventeenth century.

The manuscript upon which the Folio text of *Coriolanus* was based appears to have been pretty carefully prepared. The play is accurately divided into acts, though not into scenes, and contains rather full and explicit stage directions. The text is certainly faulty in certain places and the lines are frequently misdivided, but the proportion of error will seem small if one considers the alarming syntactic and metrical peculiarities (those of Shakespeare's last period) with which the printer had to deal. No reason has been

[1] See notes on I. i. 178, 179; II. ii. 106.
[2] Jonson's parody of II. ii. 106, however, in *The Silent Woman* is circumstantial evidence that *Coriolanus* was being acted in 1609-1610.

found for doubting that the play is wholly Shakespeare's. The text, then, as we have it, would seem
to represent a theatre manuscript fully completed by
Shakespeare and doubtless occasionally acted by his
company, but lacking evidence of the careful revision,
abridgment or amplification which popular plays
usually received.

Our actual knowledge of the production of *Coriolanus* in any form begins with 1682, when Nahum
Tate adapted the tragedy for the Theatre-Royal under
the title, *The Ingratitude of a Commonwealth: or, The
Fall of Caius Martius Coriolanus*. Tate attempted to
inject contemporary interest into the work by giving
it an application to the political troubles of the last
years of Charles II. 'Upon a close view of this
Story,' he says, 'there appear'd in some Passages no
small Resemblance with the busie Faction of our own
time. And I confess, I chose rather to set the Parallel
nearer to Sight than to throw it off at further Distance.'

Through his first four acts Tate follows Shakespeare with reasonable fidelity. The lines are mainly
Shakespeare's, though frequently refashioned, and the
chief alteration, apart from very drastic cutting, is
the quite new presentation of Valeria as 'an affected,
talkative, fantastical Lady' after the Restoration mode.
The fifth act is almost pure Tate. It develops Aufidius' Lieutenant (*Coriolanus* IV. vii.) as a melo-
dramatic villain and renegade under the name of
Nigridius, makes Aufidius an unscrupulous though un-
successful lover of Virgilia, and closes in a riot of
horror. In the final scene at 'Corioles' Menenius,
Virgilia, and young Martius are all horribly slain, as
well as Nigridius, Aufidius, and Coriolanus, while
Volumnia goes furiously mad. It is pleasing to remark
that Tate's version does not appear to have been a
success.

On November 11, 1719, the Drury Lane Theatre produced an adaptation of *Coriolanus* by John Dennis, which was printed in 1720 with the title, *The Invader of his Country: or, The Fatal Resentment.* This bad play appears to have been acted but three times. Dennis prefaced the printed edition with an indignant letter in which he expostulated against the unfairness with which the management of the theatre had treated him; but the cast, headed by Barton Booth as Coriolanus and Mrs. Porter as Volumnia, was an excellent one, and the failure of the piece to please is well accounted for by the dulness of the adaptation. The play contains extremely few lines recognizable as Shakespeare's, far fewer than Tate's revision, though it shows less than Tate's originality in inventing new plot devices. Dennis opens with the battles at Corioli and closes with a scene in which Coriolanus slays Aufidius and dies in spectacular combat with four Tribunes of the Volsci to an accompaniment of shrieks and lamentations from Volumnia and Virgilia. The most interesting scene is that of the consular election, where adherents of the candidates, Coriolanus and Sempronius, respectively, act out a lively imitation of an English electoral rally.

The theme of the play was next brought upon the English stage by James Thomson, author of the *Seasons*, whose *Coriolanus* was acted at Covent Garden some five months after the poet's death. Thomson's play is independent of Shakespeare's and follows different sources in its treatment of the legend: ignoring Plutarch, Thomson goes to the Roman historians, Livy and Dionysius of Halicarnassus, for his material. Consequently some of the characters appear with different names. Aufidius is called Attius Tullus, Coriolanus' mother Veturia, and his wife Volumnia. The mere fact that such alterations were possible shows how little the Shakespearean figures were known to the English public of the day.

Thomson's *Coriolanus* was first acted January 13, 1749, and was repeated some ten times by a very notable cast. The famous Quin took the title-rôle and Ryan the hardly less prominent or heroic part of Attius Tullus, while Peg Woffington played Coriolanus' mother and Mrs. Bellamy his wife. Thomson was the first capable English poet to touch the theme of Coriolanus since Shakespeare. His rhetorical tragedy, presenting various types of nobly sensitive souls as the eighteenth century liked to fancy them, seems to us lacking in reality and in dramatic force; but it is a worthy poem of its peculiar kind. It nowhere challenges comparison with Shakespeare, and would hardly come into the history of the latter's play, if the taste of later producers had not brought upon the stage several strange blends of Shakespeare and Thomson.

The earliest of these is ascribed to Thomas Sheridan, manager of the Smock Alley Theatre in Dublin. From thence it was transferred to Covent Garden in London, where it was produced first on December 10, 1754. There was more of Thomson than of Shakespeare in this, and Thomson's names of characters were retained. Coriolanus was played by Sheridan; Attius Tullus, Veturia, and Volumnia by the same distinguished performers who had supported those parts in the 1749 production of Thomson's tragedy. The blend of Shakespeare and Thomson, which had proved decidedly successful in Sheridan's version, became yet more so when John Philip Kemble staged at Drury Lane, February 7, 1789, another adaptation in which the greater part of the material was drawn from Shakespeare. 'In this alteration,' the *European Magazine* said at the time, 'the best parts of Shakespeare and Thomson are retained, and compose a more pleasing drama than that of either author separately.' Kemble's first three acts are wholly from Shakespeare, though much condensed; in acts four and five there is a predominance of Thomson. This piece was many times repeated. Kemble's Coriolanus and the Volumnia of his sister, Mrs. Siddons, are rated among their greatest parts; and it was in *Coriolanus* that Kemble took his leave of the stage on June 23, 1817.

On June 24, 1820, *Coriolanus,* with Shakespeare's text restored (as was a little falsely asserted), was performed at Drury Lane by Edmund Kean, whose success in this too statuesque rôle did not equal that of Kemble. Rival performances were given at Covent Garden (beginning November 29, 1819) with the title-rôle in the hands of W. C. Macready, who long continued to act the part. John Vandenhoff (from 1823) gave many successful performances of the play throughout England and Scotland, and Samuel Phelps (from 1848) at the Sadler's Wells Theatre in London. Other productions of some note in England have been those of James Anderson (from 1851), Sir Henry Irving (1901), and Sir F. R. Benson; but since the middle of the nineteenth century *Coriolanus* has had no such significance on the British stage as it enjoyed before. It was the special degree in which this play (particularly with the interpolated borrowings from Thomson) fitted the statuesque acting of Kemble and Mrs. Siddons which gave it its impetus. Its stage value suffered when the Kemble ideal of acting gave place to more romantic and perhaps more subtle conceptions.

Thomson's *Coriolanus* was played at the Southwark Theatre, Philadelphia, on June 8, 1767. The Shakespearean play—that is, presumably, the Kemble version—was first acted in the United States by the Philadelphia Company, June 3, 1796. During the latter half of the nineteenth century the American actors Edwin Booth, John McCullough, and Lawrence Barrett all distinguished themselves as Coriolanus; and the Italian Tommaso Salvini interpreted the part in Boston and other cities during the season of 1885-1886. The American actor who most identified himself with the rôle was, however, Edwin Forrest (1806-1872), whose Coriolanus was perhaps his favorite character and whose statue represents him dressed for that part.

The most notable French production of the play was that of M. Joubé at the Odéon in Paris in 1910. German performances have of late been characteristically numerous, but apparently not otherwise remarkable. In 1920 the tragedy was acted seven times in Berlin and twice at Lübeck. A total of 103 performances in different German cities has been collected for the period between 1911 and 1920.[1]

[1] See the list by Dr. E. Mühlbach, Shakespeare-Jahrbuch, 1921, pp. 159-163.

APPENDIX C

THE TEXT OF THE PRESENT EDITION

The text of the present volume is based, by permission of the Oxford University Press, upon that of the Oxford Shakespeare, edited by the late W. J. Craig. Craig's text has been carefully collated with the Shakespeare Folio of 1623, and the following deviations have been introduced:

1. The stage directions of the Folio have been restored. Necessary words and directions, omitted by the Folio, are added within square brackets.

2. Punctuation and spelling have been normalized to accord with modern English practice; e.g., anything, everything, warlike, priestlike, hostler, carcasses, scandal'd (instead of any thing, every thing, war-like, priest-like, ostler, carcases, scandall'd). Generally the changes introduced, both in punctuation and in spelling, effect a closer approximation to the Folio form. The form Martius, invariable in the Folio and in North, is restored *passim* in place of Marcius. The Folio abbreviation 'Y' are' is likewise replaced instead of the varying 'you 're,' 'ye 're,' or 'you are' of modern editions.

3. The frequent elisions, characteristic of the Folio text and often necessary for scansion of the lines, have generally been retained; e.g., th' expulsion, th' accusation, is 't, we'll, o' (for *of* or *on*), 's (for *is, his,* or *us*), etc.

4. The following changes of text have been introduced, nearly always in accordance with Folio authority. The readings of the present edition precede the colon, while Craig's readings follow it:

I. i. 29   All: First Cit.
     59   2. Cit.: First Cit. (So also in lines 67, 83,
               98, 111, 120, 127, 129, 133, 148, 153, 162,
               172.)
    116   taintingly: tauntingly
    132   you'st: you'll
ii. 30   prepar'd: prepared
iii. 3   should: would
iv. 42   follows: follow'd
vi. 6   The Roman: Ye Roman
    32   burnt: burn'd
ix. 46   an overture: a coverture

II. i. 17   Both: Sic. }
                 Bru. }
     46   Both: Bru.
    204   begin: begnaw
    212   Virgilia: Valeria
    270   their war: the war
ii. 8   hath: have
iii. 44   the: a (misprint?)
    108   bountiful: bountifully
    117   farther: further
    122   wolfish: woolvish
    123   does: do
    132   moe: more
    165   loves: love
    171   us'd: used

III. i. 65   meiny (Meynie F): many
     72   lack: lack'd
     77   their: they
    130   bosom multiplied: bisson multitude
    319   a' (a F): he
ii. 21   thwartings (things F): thwarting
    29   as little: of mettle
    113   quir'd: quired
    114   an eunuch: a eunuch
iii. 67   fold in: fold-in
    97   doth: do

IV. i. 8   home,—being: home, being
    27   'em: them
ii. 19   strook: struck (So also in IV. v. 231.)
iii. 9   appeared: approved
iv. 13   seems: seem
v. 114   an hundred: a hundred
    201   boiled: broiled

vi. 51   hath: have
     59   coming: come
vii. 28   yields: yield

V. ii. 17   verified: glorified
iii. 154   nobleman: noble man
iv. 23   'hum!': hum
v. 100   others: other

APPENDIX D

Suggestions for Collateral Reading

Plutarch's *Life of Coriolanus,* translated by North; in C. F. T. Brooke, *Shakespeare's Plutarch,* vol. ii, 137-207. London, 1909.

James Thomson: *Coriolanus.* London, 1749. Reprinted in Works of Thomson, vol. iv, Edinburgh, 1778. (See Appendix B, p. 165.)

M. W. McCallum: *Shakespeare's Roman Plays and their Background.* London, 1910.

William Hazlitt: *Characters of Shakespeare's Plays.* London, 1817. Everyman's Library edition, 1906, pp. 53-63.

Edward Dowden: *Shakspere, his Mind and Art.* 12th ed., London, 1901, chapter vi, 'The Roman Plays.'

Stopford A. Brooke: *On Ten Plays of Shakespeare.* 6th impression, London, 1919, pp. 221-252.

R. M. Alden: *Shakespeare.* pp. 286-289, New York, 1922.

An edition of *Coriolanus* in the Furness Variorum series is in preparation. The most useful annotated edition that has yet appeared is that in the Arden series, edited by W. J. Craig and R. H. Case, London, 1922. The edition in the Henry Irving Shakespeare, vol. vi, with Introduction and Notes by H. C. Beeching, is also important. Valuable commentary is to be found in the editions of W. Aldis Wright (Oxford, 1879), W. J. Rolfe (New York, 1892), and G. S. Gordon (Oxford, 1912).

INDEX OF WORDS GLOSSED

(Figures in full-faced type refer to page-numbers)

contemn: **52** (II. ii. 162)
contemning: **15** (I. iii. 47)
contriv'd: **86** (III. iii. 62)
convenient: **131** (V. iii. 191)
convented: **47** (II. ii. 59)
Corioli: **13** (I. ii. 27)
corrected: **127** (V. iii. 57)
corslet: **133** (V. iv. 22)
counsellor heart: **5** (I. i. 122)
countenance: **137** (V. v. 40)
counterfeitly: **56** (II. iii. 106)
counterpois'd: **49** (II. ii. 92)
counterseal'd: **132** (V. iii. 205)
courtesy: **130** (V. iii. 161)
coxcombs: **113** (IV. vi. 135)
coy'd: **117** (V. i. 6)
crab-trees: **41** (II. i. 207)
crack: **16** (I. iii. 74)
crafted: **112** (IV. vi. 119)
cranks: **6** (I. i. 143)
cry: **114** (IV. vi. 149)
crying confusion: **108** (IV. vi. 29)
cunning: **90** (IV. i. 9)
curbs: **3** (I. i. 74)
curdied: **127** (V. iii. 66)
cushion: **116** (IV. vii. 43)
cushions: **67** (III. i. 100)

dam: **75** (III. i. 291)
dances: **102** (IV. v. 122)
darken: **44** (II. i. 278)
darken'd: **115** (IV. vii. 5)
daws: **100** (IV. v. 47)
day: **96** (IV. iii. 32)
dear: **1** (I. i. 20)
debile: **30** (I. ix. 48)
declines: **40** (II. i. 180)
defective: **47** (II. ii. 55)
degrees: **46** (II. ii. 29)
delay the present: **25** (I. vi. 60)
deliver: **142** (V. v. 141)
demerits: **11** (I. i. 278)

designments: **137** (V. v. 35)
despite: **69** (III. i. 163)
determin'd of: **46** (II. ii. 42)
determine: **85** (III. iii. 42);
  129 (V. iii. 120)
Deucalion: **37** (II. i. 103)
devotion: **46** (II. ii. 21)
dieted: **30** (I. ix. 52)
dieted to: **119** (V. i. 58)
difference: **136** (V. v. 18)
differency: **133** (V. iv. 12)
directitude: **106** (IV. v. 223)
directly: **105** (IV. v. 197)
disbench'd: **48** (II. ii. 76)
discover: **46** (II. ii. 23)
disease: **17** (I. iii. 117)
disgrace: **4** (I. i. 99)
dislodg'd: **134** (V. iv. 45)
disposing: **116** (IV. vii. 40)
dispropertied: **44** (II. i. 267)
dissension of a doit: **97** (IV. iv. 17)
doing, beheld the: **30** (I. ix. 40)
doit: **22** (I. v. 6)
dotant: **122** (V. ii. 47)
doublets: **22** (I. v. 6)
doubt, past: **62** (II. iii. 265)
drachme: **21** (I. v. 5)
drawn your number: **62** (II. iii. 261)
duty: **126** (V. iii. 51)

effected: **29** (I. ix. 18)
embarquements: **33** (I. x. 22)
empiricutic: **38** (II. i. 130)
end (noun): **129** (V. iii. 122)
end (verb): **137** (V. v. 37)
endure: **25** (I. vi. 58)
enforce: **60** (II. iii. 227);
  83 (III. iii. 3)
engine: **133** (V. iv. 20)
enter'd: **12** (I. ii. 2)
entertainment: **96** (IV. iii. 49); **123** (V. ii. 68)

haver: **49** (II. ii. 90)
having: **122** (V. ii. 60)
havoc, cry: **74** (III. i. 273)
head, made a: **49** (II. ii. 93)
head, made new: **62** (III. i. 1)
helms: **3** (I. i. 81)
himself alone: **20** (I. iv. 51)
Hob and Dick: **56** (II. iii. 123)
holp: **111** (IV. vi. 82)
home: **49** (II. ii. 108)
home, told them: **94** (IV. ii. 48)
honest: **131** (V. iii. 166)
hopeless restitution: **63** (III. i. 16)
horn and noise: **66** (III. i. 94)
hospitable canon: **33** (I. x. 26)
housekeepers: **16** (I. iii. 56)
hum: **133** (V. vi. 23)
humorous: **35** (II. i. 52)
hungry: **127** (V. iii. 58)
hurry: **107** (IV. vi. 4)
hush'd: **131** (V. iii. 181)
huswife: **16** (I. iii. 76)
Hydra: **66** (III. i. 92)

i': **32** (I. x. 7)
in: **45** (II. ii. 15)
inches, by: **134** (V. iv. 43)
incorporate: **5** (I. i. 136)
indifferently: **46** (II. ii. 19)
infected: **139** (V. v. 72)
inform: **127** (V. iii. 71)
inherited: **42** (II. i. 217)
injurious: **86** (III. iii. 68)
innovator: **70** (III. i. 174)
insensible: **107** (IV. v. 241)
inshell'd: **109** (IV. vi. 45)
instant: **118** (V. i. 37)
instruction: **19** (I. iv. 22)
insurrection's arguing: **9** (I. i. 227)
interims and conveying gusts: **23** (I. vi. 5)

interjoin: **98** (IV. iv. 22)
interpretation: **127** (V. iii. 69)
interrupted: **73** (III. i. 248)
issues: **98** (IV. iv. 22)
itch of your opinion: **7** (I. i. 171)

Jack guardant: **122** (V. ii. 66, 67)
judicious: **141** (V. v. 128)
jump: **69** (III. i. 153)

kam: **75** (III. i. 302)
kick'd at: **50** (II. ii. 129)
kinder value: **47** (II. ii. 64)
knee: **117** (V. i. 5)

lapsing: **121** (V. ii. 19)
lay: **31** (I. ix. 82)
leads: **42** (II. i. 230); **111** (IV. vi. 83)
leasing: **121** (V. ii. 22)
left: **21** (I. iv. 54)
legs: **36** (II. i. 78)
lenity: **67** (III. i. 98)
lesson'd: **59** (II. iii. 185)
let go: **78** (III. ii. 18)
levies: **139** (V. v. 67)
lie in: **116** (IV. vii. 50)
lies: **97** (IV. iv. 8)
lies you on: **79** (III. ii. 52)
life, to the: **81** (III. ii. 106)
like: **8** (I. i. 198)
limitation: **57** (II. iii. 146)
linger: **87** (III. iii. 87)
litter'd: **73** (III. i. 238)
lockram: **42** (II. i. 228)
long of: **134** (V. iv. 33)
longs: **131** (V. iii. 170)
looks: **85** (III. iii. 29)
lots to blanks: **120** (V. ii. 10)
lurch'd: **49** (II. ii. 106)
Lycurguses: **36** (II. i. 61)

made fair hands: **112** (IV. vi. 118)

parcel: **106** (IV. v. 232)

parcels: **13** (I. ii. 32)

participate: **4** (I. i. 108)

particular: **115** (IV. vii. 13); **117** (V. i. 3)

particularise: **1** (I. i. 22)

particulars, by: **54** (II. iii. 48)

parties: **8** (I. i. 200); **76** (III. i. 313)

party, make strong: **81** (III. ii. 94)

pass this doing: **51** (II. ii. 144)

passable: **121** (V. ii. 13)

passes: **47** (II. ii. 59)

passing: **8** (I. i. 209)

passions: **98** (IV. iv. 19)

pent: **87** (III. iii. 87)

peremptory: **75** (III. i. 284)

person: **14** (I. iii. 11); **26** (I. vi. 70)

pestering: **107** (IV. vi. 7)

physical: **22** (I. v. 18)

pick: **8** (I. i. 206)

piece (noun): **85** (III. iii. 32)

piece (verb): **60** (II. iii. 220)

plainly: **125** (V. iii. 3)

plot: **81** (III. ii. 102)

points: **113** (IV. vi. 126)

policy: **79** (III. ii. 42)

poll: **68** (III. i. 133)

poll, by the: **84** (III. iii. 10)

polled: **106** (IV. v. 216)

popular: **42** (II. i. 233)

popular man: **56** (II. iii. 108)

portance: **60** (II. iii. 232)

ports: **27** (I. vii. 1); **136** (V. v. 6)

possessed: **39** (II. i. 148)

post: **138** (V. v. 50)

pot, to the: **20** (I. iv. 47)

potch: **33** (I. x. 15)

pother: **43** (II. i. 237)

pound us up: **19** (I. iv. 17)

pounds: **76** (III. i. 312)

power: **9** (I. i. 226); **12** (I. ii. 9)

practice: **91** (IV. i. 33)

prank them: **63** (III. i. 23)

prate: **130** (V. iii. 159)

precipitation: **77** (III. ii. 4)

preparation: **12** (I. ii. 15)

present: **84** (III. iii. 21)

presently: **106** (IV. v. 230)

press'd: **67** (III. i. 121)

press'd a power: **12** (I. ii. 9)

pretences: **13** (I. ii. 20)

pretext: **136** (V. v. 20)

process: **76** (III. i. 312)

progeny: **28** (I. viii. 13)

proper: **31** (I. ix. 57)

properly: **123** (V. ii. 90)

prosperous approbation: **38** (II. i. 116)

provand: **44** (II. i. 270)

prove: **25** (I. vi. 62)

psalteries: **134** (V. iv. 53)

puling: **94** (IV. ii. 52)

purge: **136** (V. v. 8)

purpos'd: **64** (III. i. 37)

purpose: **68** (III. i. 147)

put in hazard: **62** (II. iii. 264)

put . . . to 't: **51** (II. ii. 146)

put upon 't: **44** (II. i. 275)

putting on: **61** (II. iii. 260)

puts well forth: **11** (I. i. 257)

quak'd: **28** (I. ix. 6)

quarry: **8** (I. i. 204)

quir'd: **82** (III. ii. 113)

quit of: **101** (IV. v. 89)

rack'd: **117** (V. i. 16)

ranges: **71** (III. i. 205)

rapt: **102** (IV. v. 122)

rapture: **42** (II. i. 226)

rascal: **6** (I. i. 165)